SEXTUS PROPERTIUS (c. 55–15 BC) was an elegiac poet of the Augustan age, born and raised in Umbria. Little biographical detail survives beyond what can be inferred from his poems. He published his first book of verse around 30 BC, and at least three more in his lifetime. He was in the circle of the influential patron of the arts Maecenas. A successor of Catullus and rough contemporary of Vergil, Ovid and Horace, he is perhaps best known today through Ezra Pound's experimental 'homage' of 1919.

After reading Classics and Modern Languages at Merton College, Oxford, PATRICK WORSNIP worked for more than forty years as a correspondent and editor for Reuters news agency, with postings in Italy, Russia, Poland, Iran, Lebanon, the US and the UK. Since retiring in 2012, he has devoted himself to translation from Italian and Latin, and to magazine articles on Italian poetry. He divides his time between Cambridge and Umbria, Italy. He is married, with one son.

T0167893

to TRICIA
my life and travel companion

qua nebulosa cauo rorat Meuania campo,
et lacus aestiuis intepet Vmber aquis…

poems of

S E X T U S

PROPERTIUS

edited & translated by
P A T R I C K W O R S N I P

with an introduction by
Peter Heslin

Carcanet Classics

M M X V I I I

First published in Great Britain in 2018 by

Carcanet Press Ltd
Floor 4 Alliance House, 30 Cross Street
Manchester M2 7AQ

Poems, notes and afterword © Patrick Worsnip, 2018.
Introduction © Peter Heslin, 2018.

Book design: Luke Allan. Printed in England by SRP Ltd.
A CIP catalogue record for this book is available from the British
Library, ISBN 9781784106515.

The publisher acknowledges financial assistance
from Arts Council England.

Contents

Introduction *by Peter Heslin*
7

POEMS

Book One
19

Book Two
49

Book Three
101

Book Four
141

Notes
177

Afterword *by Patrick Worsnip*
241

Introduction

PROPERTIUS IS PERHAPS the most enigmatic of the great poets from the golden age of Latin literature. There are a number of reasons for this: the corruption of his Latin text as it was transmitted across the millennia; a difficult, abrupt, idiosyncratic style which demands a great deal of the reader; an obsession with mythological minutiae; and the bone-dry sarcasm with which the poet reflects upon his own vicissitudes and the politics of the day. On the one hand, Propertius seems to lack Catullus' apparent sense of immediacy and unmediated passion, while on the other, he lacks Ovid's outrageous wit. But for the connoisseur of poetry, the rewards of persevering are immense, and Patrick Worsnip's vibrant contemporary translation will bring Propertius to a new generation of discerning readers.

Propertius' distinctive contribution to love poetry is an utterly refined sense of irony. His first three books are devoted to poems narrating the ups and downs of his relationship with his girlfriend, Cynthia; he often blurs the distinction between the girl and the poetry he writes about her. He presents himself as a lover oppressed by an inescapable passion for his beloved, enslaved to her beauty and unable to write about anything else. As he invents countless variations on this basic scenario, his persona never changes. Where Catullus invites us to read his poetry as truly autobiographical and Ovid constantly lifts the mask of the earnest lover in order to wink at his readers, Propertius plays the comedic role of the absurdly obsessive lover but plays it straight. The result is poetry that presents itself as a sincere, authentic narrative of lived experience, but which is in fact a highly arch and self-ironising fiction. Propertian elegy sends up its own earnestness not by explicitly subverting its events and characters but by taking them to absurd extremes, never letting the pretence of authenticity slip.

Propertius' work belongs to the genre of Latin love elegy, which had, especially via Ovid, a vast influence upon the history of Western love poetry. The particular discourse of the genre is a first-person narrative about an obsessive love affair with a pseudonymous mistress whose beauty and wit are celebrated while her indifference, unfaithfulness and cruelty are lamented. This obsession leads to a state of voluntary slavery which causes the poet to abandon all of his serious commitments to work, family and country. The metre of elegy is borrowed from the Greeks, and consists of couplets in which the first line is a six-foot hexameter (the metre of epic) and the second is a shorter pentameter. Couplets are generally end-stopped in terms of their sense: the hexameter sets up a thought and the pentameter completes it. This format lends itself to pointed, epigrammatic expression: elegiac couplets are also the metre of epigram in antiquity.

The classical canon of Latin love elegy – Cornelius Gallus, Tibullus, Propertius and Ovid – was constructed by Ovid himself, who presents himself as its culmination and climax: 'Tibullus was your successor, Gallus, and Propertius was his; after them came I, fourth in order of time.' Ovid claims Propertius as his immediate predecessor, and Ovid is indeed Propertius' greatest disciple: he picks up those elements of Propertian elegy that are couched in an elegant irony and takes them to outrageous extremes. But Propertius would not have recognised Ovid's self-interested account of the elegiac tradition: he would have been quite furious to find himself described as Tibullus' successor. When Propertius lays out for us the poetic tradition that he saw himself belonging to, he honours Catullus and positions himself as the immediate successor of Cornelius Gallus, but he writes his rival Tibullus out of the picture entirely. All agree that Gallus was the founder of the tradition of Latin love elegy; very little of his poetry survives, though Vergil and Propertius both address him frequently in their earliest works. An important military and political figure as well as a poet, he was one of the primary lieutenants of Octavian, the man who was to become Augustus, heir of Julius Caesar and the first Roman emperor. After Octavian defeated Antony and Cleopatra and captured Egypt, he left Gallus in charge of the country, an enormously powerful and sensitive position. Before long, Gallus was accused of disloyalty and was compelled to commit suicide.

After the defeat of Antony and Cleopatra, Octavian returned to Rome and set about a programme of national renewal to celebrate and consolidate the ensuing period of peace (and absolute hegemony). As part of that programme, the regime actively solicited a new kind of verse. Augustus did not want love poetry celebrating powerful women (like Cleopatra) and the men bewitched by them (like Antony, according to the history that was written by the winners); he wanted an epic celebrating the national destiny. Before long, the regime was actively encouraging Romans to return to traditional family values and later resorted to legislation to support that aim. In this atmosphere, Latin love elegy came to stand in contrast to patriotic epic; to traditional Roman values of family, nation and masculinity; and to several of the particular obsessions of the new regime of Augustus. 'Why should I bear sons for my country's triumphs? No child of mine shall be a soldier.' When Propertius addresses these words to his mistress, swearing that he will never marry, he is pointedly rejecting the values of the new regime. This opposition between elegy and the emperor came to a head many decades later, when Ovid was exiled from Rome by Augustus; his outrageously cynical poetry about love and sex was an important factor in that punishment. Propertius himself, in his fourth and final book, moves away from an exclusive focus on love to write about Roman themes, but, given Propertius' penchant for dry humour, the extent to which this should be interpreted as marking a sea-change is disputed.

The themes of Latin love elegy can be easily enumerated, but what is more difficult is to give a sense of the qualities that set Propertius apart from the other writers in that genre. A century after Ovid, the critic and educator Quintilian revisited the canon of elegists: 'Of our elegiac poets Tibullus seems to me to be the most terse and elegant. There are, however, some who prefer Propertius. Ovid is more lascivious than either, while Gallus is more severe.' Quintilian was not often at a loss for words (this quote comes from a work in twelve books), but he seems here to be unable to capture a salient quality for Propertius in one or two adjectives, as he can easily do for the others. He simply says that 'some prefer Propertius', without being able to put his finger on quite why they do prefer him. To see what it is that has always made Propertius the choice of a select but discerning readership, it might be useful to contrast the responses of two modern poets in English who were obsessed with his work. Between them they illustrate several of the problems that have always stood in the way of appreciating Propertius and the intense appeal he holds for those who are willing to work through them.

A. E. Housman and Ezra Pound both had significant encounters with Propertius in their youth, though for very different reasons. The two poets may have briefly overlapped in Edwardian London, but they came from different worlds and were on antithetical trajectories. Housman spent his early life as a private scholar working on difficult technical problems in Latin poetry until he had accrued such an international reputation as a classical scholar that he was appointed a senior professor of Latin, first at University College London and later at Cambridge. He always regarded his own verse as a private pursuit which was secondary to his scholarship. Pound, by contrast, gave up a very brief career in academia as quickly as possible in order to cultivate a flamboyant public life as a poet. Both men were attracted by the particular difficulties and beauties of Propertius, which they sought to address in ways that were diametrically opposed.

Housman built his career as a scholar on the textual criticism of Latin poetry. Even our earliest manuscripts of ancient poetry are separated from their authors by many centuries; the texts have been copied again and again from generations of exemplars that have long been lost. The work of the textual critic is to reconstruct the original text from the conflicting evidence of the manuscripts and, where the manuscripts do not help, by force of imagination. Housman exemplified a school of thought which holds that the text of Propertius not only has localised problems; it also exhibits large-scale dislocation of couplets from their original position and places where couplets are obviously missing. Housman's early work as a scholar made his name, but it was not widely known beyond specialists until Tom Stoppard's brilliant dramatisation in *The Invention of Love* of the young Housman's struggle with Propertius: 'He's difficult – tangled-up thoughts, or, anyway, tangled-up Latin –'.

Jan Ziolkowski has recently observed that there are surprisingly few echoes of Propertius in Housman's own poetry. Indeed, they share very few themes in common. Housman's melancholic reflections on the passage of time and his evocation of the countryside as a place of lost innocence have strong echoes of Horace, Tibullus and Vergil; but Propertius is a poet of the city, of elegant salons and urban decadence. When Propertius and Cynthia go to the countryside, they are fish out of water. Housman spent much of his life working the text of Manilius, a poet he considered deeply mediocre, but that was not his view of Propertius, despite their difference in outlook. Rather, as Stoppard has seen, Housman's work on Propertius is linked with his own poetry on a deeper level: they both stand as quixotic efforts to resist and repair the passage of time. Not infrequently, however, his struggle with the forces of decay turned into a struggle with Propertius himself. Where Housman sees nonsense, others would see those genuine aspects of Propertius' style that Pound responded to: bold image and metaphor. Where to draw the line between stylistic idiosyncrasy and textual corruption – between tangled-up thoughts and tangled-up Latin – is still a matter of heated debate.

Housman never produced a critical edition of Propertius, so a truly radical, modern text has had to wait a long time. The present translation is based upon the excellent Oxford Classical Text of Stephen Heyworth, a work in the spirit of Housman, which is to say that it aims to restore a lost smoothness to the poetry, though at the risk of sometimes fixing that which was never truly broken. The reader needs to be aware that this translation is based upon a radical text, and that there is no manuscript evidence for some of its changes. One always needs to be cautious in comparing two different translations in the hope of getting a fuller picture of the meaning of the original. But that is a particular issue with Propertius, where two translations may reflect an entirely different arrangement of the underlying Latin.

Like Housman, Ezra Pound found himself engaged as a young man in a project of rearranging and rewriting Propertius. His intervention, however, took the form of a very free translation of selected passages. 'Homage to Sextus Propertius' is, in fact, not so much a translation as a new poem inspired by Propertius. Where Housman's work aimed to remove the jagged, fragmented qualities of the text as it has been transmitted to us, Pound celebrated, enhanced and exaggerated those very qualities. Pound saw Propertius' abrupt and elliptical style not as signs of damage, but as a forerunner of Modernism in general and Imagism in particular. Propertius was one of Pound's many personae: the artist as a rebel who lives for art and for love, refusing to conform to the economic and civic values of his society. Pound was particularly interested in the poems from Books Two and Three in which Propertius proclaims his aesthetic independence and his refusal to write an epic for Augustus and for his empire; it is no coincidence that those two books were written while Vergil was at work on the *Aeneid*. Where Housman's own poetry imagines Shropshire rustics singing 'God Save the Queen' as they celebrate Victoria's golden jubilee, Pound saw Propertius as a prophet of his own attitude toward the 'infinite and ineffable imbecility' of the British Empire in 1917.

The greatest contribution Pound made to our understanding of the text of Propertius was his insistence upon its pervasive irony. Victorian critics tended to read love elegy in a naively biographical mode: as the sincere expression of emotion and the narrative of real events. Classical scholars of Pound's own day did not react positively to the 'Homage', dismissing it as an inept and error-riddled translation by someone who did not know his Latin. But Pound was absolutely correct to regard the first-person voice of Propertius as a fiction, a persona, projected through an elaborately constructed mask. It was not until the 1960s, when a new generation of scholars became interested in Roman voices critical of empire and of traditional masculinity, that Pound's evocation of an ironic, anti-imperialist Propertius was rehabilitated as a prescient contribution to our understanding of the Latin poet's work.

Who then was right, Housman or Pound? Textual corruption and stylistic idiosyncrasy are not mutually exclusive explanations for the difficulty of Propertius' Latin. In that sense, both positions are correct, though where to draw the line in any particular passage will remain controversial. Pound brilliantly perceived the archness of Propertius' persona, the virulence of his criticism of Vergil's epic and his scepticism toward the emperor and his moral agenda. But he simply refused to engage with Book Four, where Propertius seems to acknowledge the greatness of the *Aeneid* and write in the national interest; the irony here is most subtle and most difficult to judge.

The trickiest aspect of Propertius for many readers is his frequent invocation of names from Greek mythology. Sometimes these are familiar and serve as straightforward illustrations of a general category: Medea the witch, Penelope the faithful wife, Orpheus the poet. Many, however, are inscrutable. For example, in Propertius' second poem of his first book he wants an example of natural, unadorned beauty, and instead of reaching for Helen of Troy he invokes the names of Phoebe, Hilaïra, Marpessa and Hippodamia. Who on earth are they? This seems at first a perverse straining after obscurity with no purpose other than showing off. Propertius' wilful obscurity can be off-putting to the reader, but he is actually doing something else. When examined closely, those four names in Elegy 1.2 have something particular in common: they all exemplify stories of a woman who was carried away on a chariot by a more powerful male rival. So on a deeper level they illustrate the real theme of that poem. Propertius tells Cynthia to shun ornament not out of his professed love of simplicity, but because he is afraid of a wealthy rival who will be able to give her expensive baubles that he cannot afford. In other words, the myths serve an ironic purpose far beyond their ostensible rhetorical purpose.

Sometimes Propertius invokes a myth that fails utterly to illustrate the point he is trying to make, and these passages can seem particularly disorienting to the reader. The answer again is Propertian irony. For example, in one poem from the second book (22a), Propertius suddenly decides that it would be a good idea to have two girlfriends. As he boasts of his potency, he compares himself to Achilles and Hector going into battle after embracing Briseis and Andromache, respectively. But the Trojan War is not the most positive paradigm for infidelity. The war started because Helen had two husbands, Menelaus and Paris, and the tragedy of the *Iliad* was precipitated by the inability of Achilles and Agamemnon to share Briseis between them. The inappropriateness of the mythology is a signal of the irony of the poem as a whole. We know that Propertius' idea of two-timing Cynthia will end in a disaster, so the Trojan War is actually a good parallel for what will happen: we have learned that Cynthia's anger is as savage as Achilles'. In Propertius' imagined threesome, he will not play the role of Achilles or Hector, but of Briseis. Another myth earlier in that same poem also functions ironically. Propertius says that even if he were as blind as the poet Thamyras, he would never be blind to pretty girls. This seems to be nothing more than the invocation of a needlessly obscure myth until one examines it more closely. The reason for Thamyras' blindness was that he challenged the Muses to a singing contest. If he won, he got to sleep with as many of them as he liked; if they won, they could do with him as they wished. He lost, and the Muses plucked out his eyes. Thus Propertius' apparently off-hand reference to the blindness of Thamyras encodes a prediction of what really happens to a poet who proposes polyamory to his Muse/girlfriend. The poet's confident claim that he can handle more than one girl-friend is sustained with a straight face throughout the poem; the irony is only revealed by close examination of its mytho-logical references.

The myths that pepper Propertius' texts are not the mean-ingless products of a sterile rhetorical training, nor are they distancing gestures, invocations of timeless clichés; they are integral to the poems and are often the key to unpicking their irony. This close connection between myth and life is vividly illustrated in Propertius' very first elegy. Vergil had included two poems in his pastoral *Eclogues* that situated the 'real' poet Cornelius Gallus in imaginary mythical landscapes, where he consorts with Apollo and other gods, nymphs, and so on. Propertius picked up on this half-mythologised aspect of the final poem of Vergil's collection, and fully mythologised the love elegist under the guise of Milanion, who in an obscure version of the myth was the lover of the mythical huntress Atalanta. Like Vergil, Propertius playfully mingles the timeless world of myth and the present day by saying that Milanion's adventures happened 'recently' (*modo*). For Housman, this was a logical impossibility, and he postulated that a couplet must have dropped out here with another instance of *modo* that would have changed its meaning; this is the position adopted by Heyworth. But I think this is to miss Propertius' point, which was to overlay the distant mythical past and the immediate present in such a way as to signal the importance of this tactic to his readers from the outset.

There is another coordinating *modo* in Propertius' work, but it does not lie in a couplet lost from his first elegy. It comes years later, at the very end of his second book, when he once again reflects upon the situation of Cornelius Gallus, who has recently (*modo*) been forced to commit suicide by the emperor. Propertius tells a polite lie, implying that it was from the wounds of love that he perished, then passing on the baton of love elegy to Propertius; this is where Pound ends his 'Homage'. In Stoppard's play, the fictional Housman also quotes this couplet as he reflects upon the 'invention of love', which is to say the inception of the Western tradition of love poetry, by Catullus, Cornelius Gallus and Propertius: '*Lately. Modo. Just recently.* They were real people to each other, that's the thing ... Apollo there in person, but you can trust it, that's what I mean ...' This is the paradox of Propertian elegy. It is profoundly rooted in the everyday experiences of real people living lives, but the poems describe highly arch, theatrical scenarios. Myth is often the point where the apparently breathless earnestness of the first-person lover meets the ironic artifice of the poet.

The raw material of Propertian elegy consists of the emotions, situations and difficulties in love affairs that are common to humankind, but the particular scenarios depicted in the elegies are highly wrought fictions in which the first-person narrator is often of dubious reliability. The relationship between art and life in Propertius is illustrated by a famous painting Propertius alludes to in an elegy (II.3) in which he tries to give an impression of the beauty of his Cynthia. Zeuxis was one of the most famous painters of ancient Greece, and his masterpiece, a portrait of Helen of Troy, later came to hang in Rome. The story of its genesis, as told by Cicero and others, is that the painter could not find one woman beautiful enough to be the model for his Helen, so he painted a composite portrait, combining the most beautiful features from a multitude of models. This, hints Propertius, is the way he created Cynthia, the woman and the poetry about her: as a composite fictional synthesis based upon fragments of reality. Propertius was not only involved in the 'invention of love', as one of the founders of the most influential genre of love poetry in the history of Western literature; he was also one of the inventors of autobiography as a genre of poetic fiction.

Peter Heslin
Professor of Classics, Durham University

BOOK ONE

I.1

Cynthia was first, her eyes
made me her abject prisoner-of-war.
I had till then been untouched by Amor,
who now pulled down the vanity of my glance,
trampled my head with his feet.
That villain taught me to despise
respectable girls and lead an aimless life.
It's a year now this lunacy won't leave me,
the whole pantheon ranged against me.

Tullus, you've read that Milanion shirked nothing
to break down the contempt of Atalanta.
He roamed demented through Arcadian wilds,
killed beasts, was wounded by the centaur's club,
made the rocks echo with his moans ...
And so tamed the girl sprinter,
such is the power of word and deed in love.

My slow-witted passion can think up no such tricks,
the map from the past is forgotten.
But you who claim you can bring down the moon
and appease spirits with magic fires,
now's your chance! Change the mind of my beloved,
let her pallor exceed mine!
Then I'll believe you can summon
stars and ghosts with your witches' songs.

And you, my friends, too late to stop my fall,
fetch first aid at least for a sick heart.
Scalpel, cautery, I'll bear it all
with fortitude – just give me
the freedom to say what anger dictates.
Take me across the sea, to the furthest lands,
where no woman will know where I travel.

But you stay here, whose prayers the god has heard,
live for ever in safe, requited love.
The Venus I know torments me through the night,
a love never unemployed or absent.
Shun this malediction, I tell you:
let each hold to his own, and though
the feeling grows familiar, not move on.

Listen to my advice. Don't hesitate,
or you'll recall these words with pain. Too late!

I.2

What's the sense, darling, going out
in a fancy coiffure, swinging the sheer pleats
of an outfit from Kos, plastering your hair
with oriental 'product'? Imported finery
makes *you* the product.
Commercial artifice ruins nature's assets,
masks your body's innate lustre.
No concoction will enhance your figure,
believe me. Amor is naked, unadorned,
and has no love for beauty salon contrivers.

Undug earth still sends up
a profusion of colours, ivy comes better
left to its own devices, finer specimens
of arbutus grow in remote valleys, streams
don't have to study what course to follow.
Common pebbles dot the prettiest beaches.
Ever hear of birds taking singing lessons?

It wasn't their dress sense that caused Leucippus' daughters
to give Castor and Pollux the hots,
or set lustful Apollo and Idas
at odds over Marpessa;
Hippodamia needed no cosmetics
to catch the eye of the foreign suitor
and get driven away in his chariot.
Jewellery was superfluous to their faces,
their complexions out of Apelles' paintings.
They put no thought into winning lovers worldwide,
their beauty enough to shed their virginity.

I worry you might rate me lower than rivals:
pleasing one man is all
the make-up a woman needs,
seeing how Apollo gave you his gift of song,
Calliope skill on the lyre in abundance,
and how grace and wit roll off your tongue,
and Minerva and Venus would give you their seal of approval.
Such arts ensure you my undying love
(so long as you quickly tire of cheap luxuries).

I.3

On Naxos, Ariadne
comatose on the empty sand
while Theseus' ship dwindles into nothing;
Andromeda gorging on her first sleep,
free now from the unforgiving rock;
a Thracian maenad, danced out,
tumbled on the grass beside the river.

Cynthia, head on outsplayed fingers
and breathing quietly, could be one of these
as I stumble in, the worse for drink,
and the servants' torches gutter. It is late.
Not yet incapable, I weave
towards the couch her body lightly imprints;
Eros and Bacchus – neither to be denied –
fill me with their respective fires: just tuck
your arm, they order, gently beneath her frame,
press lips to lips, take sword in hand and …

Can't do it. Daren't disturb her rest.
She can be savage. I know her tongue's lash.
Instead I hover, gawping like Argus
at the horns that sprang from Io.
And, Cynthia, I put my garland on your brow,
amuse myself arranging your stray hair,
balance apples furtively on your cleavage,
only to see my largesse roll away:
sleeper's ingratitude!
Your every sigh,
every slight tremor has me terrified;
it means bad dreams trouble your head
– someone taking you by force …

The moon marching past the shutter slats,
the busy moon, its light lingering too long,
opens her eyes. She speaks, propped on one elbow:
'Back home to bed with me? She turned you out, then?
How nasty of her! So, where was it,
the place you spent the night you'd promised me?
Look at you, fit for nothing and the stars set.
You bastard! I'd like you to pass
a few nights the way you expect of me.
I tried to stay awake with needlework,

playing snatches of music as I drooped.
Just the occasional complaint, sitting alone,
that you were *quite* so long in that woman's arms.
That was my last thought as I lay back crying,
before sleep nudged me with its soothing wings.'

I.4

Why with your paeans for multifarious girls
are you trying, Bassus, to force me
to dump my own true-love and find another?
Why not allow me the rest of my life
in familiar servitude?

You could laud Antiope's profile,
sing the praises of Spartan Hermione, perhaps;
the finest examples of that Age of Beauty
are undistinguished next to Cynthia.
So how could she lose in the harshest court of judgment
against the third-rate 'lovelies' that you mention?

Her figure is the least part of my passion;
there's other things to die for, Bassus:
her fresh complexion, the grace of her body movement,
the pleasures I enjoy discovering
beneath the reticence of her dress ...
The more you seek to sabotage our love,
the more we frustrate you with our constancy.

Your comeuppance looms: she'll be livid when she hears;
you've made an enemy, one who won't be silent;
Cynthia won't let me see you, or look you up
herself; she won't forget this outrage;

she's going to go round all the girls in town,
bad-mouthing you: every door will be slammed shut.

There's no altar she won't weep on,
no sacred stone.
There's nothing that tries Cynthia more sorely
than her beauty going to waste because love is stolen –
especially mine. May it always be so,
may I never find anything to complain of in her.
So *basta!* with your envious, spiteful jibes:
we'll keep on the road we're travelling, side-by-side.

I.5

Are you off your head, Gallus?
You actually *want* the purgatory I put up with?
Prepare, then, to know ultimate hardships, my friend,
walk through unimaginable fires,
drain all the toxic potions in Thessaly.

Cynthia's not one of those easy-come, easy-go girls:
she's not one to get angry with you *nicely*.
Even when she's ready to gratify you,
she'll have a thousand hassles up her sleeve!
She won't let you sleep or take your eyes off her:
she ties men down with her moody fits.

I can see you now at my door when she's turned you away,
your words of bravado failing as you snivel,
hands shaking, fear
leaving its ugly mark upon your features,
not able to spit out your sorry story,
not knowing who you are or where!

You'll learn then the harsh terms of my girl's service,
and what exclusion means.
You'll understand the whiteness in my face,
why I seem shrivelled in my body.
Don't imagine your ancestry can help your love life.
Love has no time for dusty oil-paintings.

Let the slightest hint of your folly go public,
and your noble name's an instant piece of gossip!
Don't expect any remedy from me then,
when I don't have a cure for my own ailment;
fellow sufferers from a common love,
we'll weep on each other's shoulders ...

So don't ask, Gallus, what Cynthia is capable
of doing: when she says yes, it's your funeral.

I.6

To cross the Adriatic with you, Tullus,
would be just fine, spread sail on the Aegean;
together we could climb Arctic mountain ranges,
or travel south to see the Ethiopians.
What holds me back? My girl's arms and her tongue,
her white-faced rages, her insistent pleading.

She rattles on all night about her passion,
how my leaving would prove gods don't exist;
I don't love her, she says, running through the list
of what angry girlfriends do to ungrateful men.
One hour of this complaining is my limit:
A laid-back relationship? Forget it!

Why bother going to Athens to read philosophy,
or visiting Asia Minor's monuments,
if as soon as anchor's weighed Cynthia starts
madly scratching my face and abusing me,
claiming storm-delay's the sole reason for my kisses
and the supreme evil is male fecklessness?

Go and pave the way for your uncle's prestigious posting,
restore the rule of law to forgetful allies.
From your boyhood you never had much time for loving –
the nation's defence topped your priorities.
Let's hope the cherub spares you my troubles,
everything at the root of my distress.

Fate always wanted me horizontal:
let me resume perpetual profligacy.
Many have gladly lived and died as lovers –
may my headstone record me among their number.
I wasn't born for glory or battle:
destiny drafted me into another army.

You, perhaps, will be in easy-living Ionia,
where the Pactolus washes the fields with gold-dust;
but whether you tramp the land or plough the sea,
you'll be part of the imperial success story.
Think of me once in a while for a few minutes,
and know for sure that the stars frown on me.

I.7

You're deep into ancient Thebes, Ponticus,
the horrors of fratricidal war –
rivalling old Homer, I would swear,

(if history's as kind to your work as to his).
I'm grappling, as usual, with love poems, searching
for the *mot juste* for a demanding woman:
ten percent inspiration, ninety percent vexation,
as I chronicle the trials of my life.

That's how I spend my days, it's what I'm known for,
that's how I hope to build a reputation.
The spurned lover can pore over my verse,
maybe learning something from my troubles,
impressed that I regularly pleasured a girl of letters,
Ponticus (and put up with undeserved tantrums).

If The Lad picks *you* off with a well-aimed bowshot
(you really shouldn't have insulted the gods I serve!),
your camps, your seven armies will seem a world away,
unresponsive, immobile. You'll be sorry then!
You'll wish, vainly, you could write elegiacs,
but love will have come too late to prompt your pen.

You'll be amazed I'm considered a leading poet,
the preferred reading of Rome's literati;
young lovers will be bound to say as they pass my tomb:
'Laureate of our passion, are you really dead?'
So don't you scorn my songs so high-mindedly:
fame can pay a big bonus when delayed.

I.8a

You've gone mad, then.
Our love doesn't hold you back?
The freezing Balkans are preferable to me?
This Mr. What's-his-name is such a catch

you'll leave me and go off wherever the wind blows?
You don't mind hearing a furious sea howl,
tough enough to make your bed on a ship's planks?
You feel like trampling frost with your delicate feet,
trudging through snow we don't get in Rome,
Cynthia?

I long for the winter storms to rage twice over,
sailors killing time as the Pleiades loiter,
ropes not to be cast off from Italy's shores,
my prayers not to float away on a hostile breeze,
leaving me rooted on an empty beach,
calling you cruel, shaking my angry fist.

But still,
however you've treated me, promise-breaker,
let the sea-nymphs not frown upon your journey,
favourable winds not die and becalm you once
your ship is under way;
and when you've safely rounded Karaburun,
let the placid waters of Orikum receive you.
Don't worry: marriage torches won't tempt me
to stop cursing my luck at your doorway,
darling.
I won't stop asking sailors hurrying past:
'Tell me the port where my girl's being kept.'
'She can follow Jason and the Argonauts
to the Black Sea and back, she'll still be mine,'
I shall say.

I.8b

She'll stay! She's promised! Screw my enemies!
I've won: she gave in to my insistent pleading.
Malicious lechers, drop your gleeful fantasies:
Cynthia's not going anywhere right now.

She's crazy about me, and besotted with Rome
for my sake; for me, she'd turn down a king's ransom.
She prefers to cuddle up in my single bed,
she just wants to be mine – any old how –
even if offered all the riches horse-breeding
Elis won or the dowry of Hippodamia.

He gave her much and promised her the world;
greed did not make her, though, run from my arms.
It wasn't gold or Indian pearls
that swayed her, just the eloquence of sweet poems.

Apollo speeds to the lover's aid. Muses exist.
To keep precious Cynthia mine, I relied on them.
Mine, mine, mine, day or night!
I can touch the highest stars with outstretched palms.
No rival can filch a love as strong as this:
that will be my boast until my hair goes white.

I.9

Didn't I tell you, Ponticus,
love would come for you, mocker,
ending your freedom of speech?
Look how, tongue-tied and obedient,
you bend to a girl's orders,

she who had been in your pocket
can now make you do any bidding.

Dodona's prophetic pigeons
can't rival me in love forecasts,
which girl will subdue which boy;
tears of pain have made me
the expert; how I would rather
be shot of this love, and a novice!

So much for your weighty epic
lamenting Thebes' lyre-built ramparts.
In affairs of the heart it's Mimnermus
whose verses count more than Homer's:
Love's a softie and likes gentle poems.
File those tragic books in your top drawer,
write something a girl would enjoy!
No material at hand? Are you crazy?
You're divining for water in mid-stream.

You've still got the pallor, the real fire
to come, all you've felt is the first spark.
Soon you'll opt for India's tigers
for company, your relaxation
being strapped to a wheel in hell,
rather than feel The Lad's darts
coursing through your bone marrow,
'yes, darling' to her every tantrum.
Love gives you wings with one hand,
just to pin you to earth with the other…

Don't be fooled that she seems compliant:
once you possess her, it's claws out,
she's filling your field of vision,
no other door to knock at.

Love steals on you unawares
until his hand's on your windpipe:
whoever you are, beware
of his fast talk. The decent thing
is first to acknowledge your error:
putting a name to your malady
is often, in love, some comfort.

I.10

That magic night when you and she
made out, Gallus (I was there
to witness your erotic tears)!
Magic remembering that night
still summoned in my fantasy:
I saw her enfold you, saw you die,
your words becoming slow, strung out.
Sleep weighed my eyes down, the blushing
moon's chariot halfway through the sky,
but I was transfixed by your sport,
such was the fire in your love-talk.

You took me in your confidence,
accept this gift for that pleasure:
not just a poem of your affair,
friendship can give something more.
I can splice parted lovers again,
open a woman's slammed-shut door,
I can heal fresh amorous wounds
with the strong medicine in my pen.
Cynthia taught me what to shun
or follow: fruits my own love bore.

No fights with her when she's down,
no harsh words or long silences,
denying her wish with a frown,
ignoring something kind she said.
A put-down rouses her resentment,
a hurt perpetuates her anger;
the more you're loving and patient,
the more you will be rewarded.
To stay content with one lover,
wear the chains, fill your heart with her.

I.11

While you holiday in summery Baia, Cynthia,
where Hercules' causeway stretches along the shore,
and admire how the sea in the Bay of Naples
has lately been channelled into Lake Averno –
do thoughts of me enter your head sometimes at night?
Does love flicker in some corner of your heart?
Or has a rival, pretending to adore you,
stolen you, Cynthia, from your place in my poems?
When the cat's away … a girl tends to forget
those solemn pledges she made …

I'd rather you were idling in a dinghy
with tiny oars on Lake Lucrino,
or confined to that narrow pool at Cuma,
one arm after the other gliding through the water,
than draped languidly on a quiet beach, listening
in no hurry to some man's plausible whispers.

Of course, I *trust* you, your reputation is ironclad …
but love always trembles in this situation.

Forgive me, then, if these lines bring you
any note of gloom: you can blame my fears.
I could not care more for my adored mother,
or take any thought for my life if you were not here.
You are my home, Cynthia, you are both
my parents, my delight all of the time.
If I'm happy or sad when I call on friends,
whatever I am, I say: 'It's Cynthia.'

Just leave rotten Baia as soon as you can:
those beaches will separate many couples,
beaches inimical to faithful girls.

To hell with the waters of Baia, an insult to love!

I.12

Ah Rome, stop charging me with idleness –
I'm just killing time while Cynthia's not here.
She's about as many miles from my bed
as the Volga from the Po;
without her embrace
my customary fires remain unfuelled,
none of her sweet nothings tinkling in my ear.

I was favoured before: no one was ever
so confident in a love affair.
Men envied me: am I now in some god's sights?
Some oriental herb separating us?
Travel changes women:
I'm not what I once was
to her. How much love has vanished in a trice!
Now I have to spin out the long nights
on my own, bore myself with my own voice.

Weeping's a joy when she's there to hold:
love relishes being sprinkled with tears;
or else to switch your passion if she goes cold –
taking your slavery elsewhere has its pleasures.
But I can't love another or leave her:
Cynthia was first; last will be Cynthia.

I.13

Typically of you, Gallus,
        you'll exult at my misfortune
                now my love has been snatched away and I'm
                                single.
I won't reciprocate
        your disloyal talk:
                I hope your girl never cheats on you, Gallus.
For while your reputation
        grows for deceiving girls
                and sure-footedly wasting no time in any affair,
you've lost your head to *someone*;
        at last you look pale – just
                one slip and you're off the track already.
This one is punishment for
        the pain you ignored in the others:
                she'll exact payment in misery on their behalf.
She'll put a stop to those
        quick-fire affairs of yours;
                your free ride in quest of novelty's about to end.
I'm not going on malicious rumours
        or horoscopes: I've *seen* you.
                Can you deny my eyewitness testimony?
I saw you melt with her arms
        clasped round your neck, I saw

your tears, Gallus, your hands' lengthy
explorations,
your longing to lay down your soul
on her voluptuous lips ...
and what followed, my friend, I am too polite to
mention ...
I could not have prised
you apart, such was the
demented fury between the pair of you.

You outstripped Neptune when,
in the guise of a river of Thessaly,
he overwhelmed the unresisting Tyro;
you surpassed the first joys
of Hercules when his funeral
pyre turned to flames of love for Hebe in heaven.
One day has left all past
amours in the dust: the torch
she has set beneath you is white-hot;
she put an end to your old
vanity – it's over:
you're a prisoner of your own passion.
No wonder, when she's a prize
for Jupiter, rival to Leda
and Leda's two daughters, lovelier than all three.
Perhaps more alluring than all
the heroines of ancient Greece,
her conversation able to make Jove love her.
But since you're about – for once –
to die of love, make the most of it:
this was the portal reserved for you.
May this unwonted mistake
turn out well for you,
and all the women you want enjoy in her.

I.14

I think of you, Tullus, lounging beside the Tiber,
imbibing fine wines from a silver cup,
watching the racing yachts go scudding past
or the barges lumber along, towed by rope;
the trees in the grove you planted tower up
high as the forests of the Caucasus.
These things cannot compete, though, with Amor:
my love and boundless riches – it's no contest.

Whether she spins out a night I'd hungered for
or spends a day of easy love with me,
Asian rivers wash bullion to my house,
I pluck the pearls from under the Red Sea;
kings surrender to me in the wars of joy –
may it last until fate tells me it's time to die!
When Amor's against you can money be a pleasure?
I want no rewards if I face the scowl of Venus.

That goddess can shatter the strength of mighty heroes,
inflict pain on even the toughest mind;
fearlessly cross a Carrara marble doorway,
slip into a bed of cloth of gold, Tullus,
make a young man twist all night in agony:
bright silken fabrics can bring no solace.
I shall fear no kingdoms, as long as she is kind,
and even despise the gifts of Alcinous.

I.15

I have long expected the worst from your fecklessness,
but never, Cynthia, this perfidy.
Look at the danger fortune lands me in!
Yet you are slow to arrive in my distress.
You must fix your hair (which was styled yesterday)
and put your make-up on (which takes forever).
There are Eastern jewels you need for your bust-line ...
Dolling yourself up, perhaps, for a new lover?

Not exactly Calypso, rocked by Ulysses' leaving,
when she wept long ago to the deserted ocean:
her hair was not done at all as she sat grieving
for days on end, reproaching the unjust sea,
and though she sorrowed she would never be
with him again, was glad for their past devotion.

Nor exactly Hypsipyle, distraught in her empty
bedroom when the winds took Jason away;
after him she never felt again the fire
that had melted her for the guest from Thessaly.
Or Evadne, who died on her husband's funeral pyre,
a byword throughout Greece for her constancy.

None of these examples managed to reform
your character and make you a glorious legend.
Stop those words, Cynthia, repeating old perjuries.
The gods have let them pass, don't make things worse.
The gall of it! Were it you at risk of harm,
I'd be the one to suffer if something happened!
Rivers will sooner flow back from their estuaries
and the year parade the seasons in reverse
than the love in my heart will turn to ill intent:
be what you want, I can't be indifferent.

Don't put such a low price on those eyes
that made me believe your falsehoods time and again!
You swore if you had told me any lies
they would fall out into your cupped fingers:
can you now lift them up to the great sun,
not trembling, conscious of the wrong you've done?
Who forced you to blench a dozen pallid colours
or wet your cheeks with those reluctant tears?
So I die now, my last message to lovers:
have no trust in the blandishments of women!

I.16

I was once a door thrown wide for victorious warriors,
dedicated to the goddess of chastity;
gilded chariots lined up at my threshold,
prisoners-of-war drenched me with tears of entreaty …

Look at me now:
dented by the nocturnal brawls of drunks,
groaning under the pounding of low-class hands;
withering flowers hang off me,
spent torches mark where a shut-out lover waited.

And how can *I* defend the resident lady
from scandalous gossip? All
I'm famous for is rude graffiti these days.
Grinding complaints would have me burst into tears,
or – worse – the long vigil of one particular suppliant,
who won't let my posts rest in peace
with his serenades of penetrating eloquence:

'Door, you're crueller even than your owner,
standing there, your hard panels closed and dumb.
You never slide back your bolts to admit my suit
or are moved to pass on my *sotto voce* pleading.
No end, then, to my ordeal,
sleeping rough on the step's residual warmth?
Midnight pities my recumbent form,
the stars setting, the wind chilled by dawn frost.

'You never had much time for human misery,
never answered back from your silent hinges.
If only my voice could percolate through
some chink into my darling's pretty ears.
She may be tougher than granite, iron or steel,
but she'd not stay dry-eyed,
involuntary teardrops would well up.
Now she rests on another well-satisfied arm,
and my words fall by the wayside in the night-wind.

'Unique and supreme cause of my misfortune,
door unimpressed by my presents,
impervious to the petulance of my tongue
(given to wounding jokes when I've been drinking).
You let me rant on till I lose my voice,
waiting out anxious hours at the street corner;
yet I write poems for you in the latest style,
even bend to press kisses on your steps.
How many times have I knelt before you, traitor,
giving you offerings with furtive hands.'

Etcetera. The repertoire of woebegone lovers,
in competition with the dawn chorus.
Between the owner's vice and her lover's voice,
it's hard to say which brings me more ill repute.

I.17

And justly, since I sailed away from you,
my interlocutors are passing seagulls;
Cassiope's setting has not launched my ship,
my prayers fall on an unhearing shore.

You command the winds from far off, Cynthia,
the vicious threats muttered by the gale are yours.
What chance of this storm dying down?
Who would have thought it – a tomb on this patch of sand?

Sweeten your harsh complaints: the darkness,
the shoals can sate your thirst to punish me.
Could you contemplate my mortality dry-eyed,
not clutching my remains against your bosom?

Damn him who first constructed boats and rigging
and journeyed on the unwelcoming sea!
Better far to have sat out her tempers
(one girl in a million in that too)
than view this beach, hemmed by uncharted woods,
the Gemini eluding my blank stare.

At home, if death had buried my pain,
a last stone marking love's resting place,
she would have offered her hair for my casket,
I should have lain on roses strewn by her;
She would have called my name over my ashes,
so earth would not weigh on me.

                                But, you daughters
of the princess of the ocean, now unfurl
our white sails with your dance;

if love ever glided down to touch your waves,
preserve a fellow soul for kinder shores.

I.18

No question it's lonely here,
a quiet place for a moan,
as a westerly breeze takes hold of the empty copse.
Perfect for freely venting repressed grudges,
(if the rocks can keep a secret).

Where to begin, Cynthia, your fit of pique?
The exact point, Cynthia, when
you triggered my weepy mode?
One of the lucky lovers,
they used to call me:
loving you proved to be the blot on my record.

Just deserts? Name the charges that changed your mind.
A new girl causing you grief?
Would you come back to me if
I said no other woman
had laid her pretty feet across my doorstep?
I owe you a hard time for my misery,
but I won't get so incensed I provoke
your righteous indignation,
those eyes all swollen from crying.

Maybe I'm not looking lovelorn –
no change of complexion,
a certain lack of sincerity in my face?
These trees can bear witness – they're experts on love,
the beech, the fir that Pan fancied –

to how my words echo in their soft shade,
'Cynthia' carved on their bark!
Or could my distress at your maltreatment of me
have caused it (but that's only known
to your door – and he's not talking)?

Cravenly I've got used
to obeying your haughty orders,
no complaints or tearful outbursts.
My reward? These thorn-covered hills and chilly rocks,
restless sleep on an overgrown track;
and any tale of woe I care to tell
is strictly for the trilling birds.
Be how you like, I shall still make
the woods resound with 'Cynthia',
your name never lost in the bare boulders.

I.19

I am not now afraid of death,
                              Cynthia;
the due day, the funeral pyre,
                    I'm ready for it.

But that you might not love me when I'm gone –
that fear is worse than the end of life itself.
I did not fall in love so casually
that it can vanish, forgotten
                              when I'm dust.

The hero Protesilaus,
                  even in the underworld murk,
could not stop remembering

                    the wife who had been his joy,
but came, a ghost, to his old home,
longing to clasp her with insubstantial hands.

Whatever I'll be in the afterlife,
I'll be yours even as a spirit:
great love can transit the frontiers of death.
Let them come *en masse*,
                          the beautiful widows of Troy
that fell as plunder to the men of Greece –
not one will outshine you in my eyes,
                                Cynthia.

And even if (as may Earth grant in fairness)
a long old age awaits you,
when you join me I shall still love you
                                and weep.
Could you, in life, feel that from my embers?
Then death, wherever it comes,
                            will not taste sour.

My fear is you'll forget my tomb,
                          Cynthia,
distracted from my dust by cruel Amor,
compelled (against your will)
                        to dry your tears:
relentless pressure can bend a girl's firmest resolve.

So while we may, let us exult in love
that never can be long enough.

I.20

In the name of my undying love for you, Gallus, this piece
of advice – don't let it slip from your vacuous mind.

Cruel fortune often frowns on the incautious lover,
as the Argonauts found to their cost at the River Ascanius.
You burn for a Hylas resembling the one in this story,
sharing his name and rivalling him in beauty.
Exploring the sacred streams of wooded Umbria,
dipping your toe in the water of the Aniene,
pacing the giants' beach in the Bay of Naples –
wherever a wandering river is your host,
protect that boy from the grasping hands of nymphs
(our Italian ones are no less lustful).
Or else it's barren mountains and freezing boulders
for you, Gallus, not to mention uncharted lakes.
That's what Hercules had to endure as he wandered weeping
in foreign lands. (The Ascanius was unmoved.)

The story: once upon a time, the good ship Argo
slipped out of dock in Thessaly on the long voyage
to Colchis, glided through the Dardanelles
and anchored off the rocks of Mysia.
Our band of heroes, disembarking on the calm shore,
covered the beach with piles of soft foliage.
Hercules' companion, though, had gone further to find
precious water supplies from a secluded spring.
The two sons of the North Wind followed him,
Zetes sometimes in the lead, sometimes Calais,
hovering as they homed in to snatch kisses
or taking turns to plant them upside down:
he mocks them as they hang on wing-tip,
beats off the flying ambush with a branch.

And they're gone ...
But Hylas – *hélas!* – was heading towards the dryads.

The spring was under the crest of Mount Arganthus,
a desirable water home for the local nymphs;
above it dew-flecked apples
hung, uncultivated, from wild trees,
lilies sprang all round from the flooded meadow,
white among crimson poppies.
The boy, clipping them off with his fingernails,
puts flowers ahead of his appointed task;
he leans, insouciant, over the pretty pool,
spinning out his mission to admire the reflections.

At last he dips his hands to collect the water,
leaning on his right arm for a full measure.
Fired by his beauty, the dryad girls
stopped their usual dances in amazement;
he slipped, they pulled him easily into the water,
the splash of his body the only sound he made.
Far away, Hercules calls three times, 'Hylas'; the only
answer the breeze brings: the name off the distant mountains.

Be warned, Gallus, and take care of your love:
don't trust those nymphs with a gorgeous Hylas again.

I.21

Soldier wounded in the siege of Perugia,
    hurrying to avoid the fate I suffered,
why do your eyes stare as you turn, hearing my groan?
    I'm on your side, one of the same army.
I hope you survive to gladden your parents with your
                               homecoming:
    just let my sister hear your tearful account –
how I eluded the blades of Octavian's swords,
    but not the hands of unknown assassins;
she'll find many bones scattered on the Apennine
    ridges, but should know that these are mine.

I.22

Who I am, where I'm from, what is my family,
    you often ask me, Tullus, as a friend.
You know the tombs of Perugia that scar our land,
    Italy's burial place in her time of trouble,
when Roman discord drove her citizens to ruin.
    Etruria's dust brought me my private sorrow,
allowing the body of my kinsman to lie abandoned
    with no earth to cover up his bones.
Where it comes closest to the fields below the city,
    the fertile soil of Umbria gave me birth.

BOOK TWO

II.1

You ask why I keep writing about love,
why folk recite this unmanly verse of mine.
It's not Calliope or Apollo dictating it to me:
the girl herself is my sole inspiration.
Does she promenade in gleaming silk from Kos?
A whole volume will be about her dress.
Did I see her stroll with a lock straying down her forehead?
It makes her proud to go out when her hairstyle's praised.
When she strikes song from the lyre with ivory fingers,
I'm amazed at how her hands make art seem easy;
when she lets her eyelids droop in search of sleep,
I find a thousand new causes for poetry;
when she tears off all her clothes to engage with me,
ah, think of the long Iliads we compose.
In short, whatever it is she's done or said,
a historical epic can grow out of ... nothing!

Maecenas, if fate had given me the power
to lead bands of heroes into combat,
I wouldn't write of Titans, or how giants piled
mountains on each other to build a road to heaven,
or ancient Thebes, or Troy that made Homer famous,
how Xerxes linked two seas with a canal,
Romulus' reign, the arrogance of towering Carthage,
the threats of the Cimbri and how Marius defeated them ...
I'd record the martial feats of your friend Augustus,
and you, after him, would be my second theme.
If I wrote of Modena, the civil strife at Philippi,
the rout off Sicily in the naval clash,
the ruined homes of the ancient Etruscan race,
the captured shores of Ptolemy's lighthouse island,
Egypt and the Nile, when its seven streams
were humbled, taken to Rome in effigy,
when gold chains hung around the necks of kings

and the prows of Actium rolled down the Sacred Way –
my muse would weave you into those tales of war,
Maecenas, ever loyal whether peace comes or goes.

Callimachus, though, doesn't have the lung-power
to sing of Jupiter's showdown with the giant,
nor can my chest summon the thunderous tones
to trace Augustus back to his Trojan forebears.
The sailor talks of winds, the ploughman of oxen;
the soldier counts his wounds, the shepherd sheep;
my kind fight their battles between the sheets:
let's all devote our days to the skills we excel in.
Dulce et decorum est in amore mori;
sweet too to enjoy one love: may I always do so,
even if I have to drink Phaedra's potions
that failed to work upon her stepson,
even if I have to die of Circe's herbs
or Medea heats her cauldron on the fire.
Since one woman has taken my feelings hostage,
my funeral cortege will start from her home.

All human ailments have their own medicine;
only for love there is no specialist.
Machaon cured Philoctetes' paralysed legs,
the centaur Chiron healed the eyes of Phoenix;
the doctor god restored with Cretan herbs
dead Androgeon to his father's home;
young Telephus, wounded by Achilles' spear,
received the remedy from the self-same blade.
Anyone who can rid me of my affliction
will be able to put the fruit in Tantalus' hand,
or fill the leaky jars with the Danaids' pots
to spare their delicate necks from all that water,
or free Prometheus from the Caucasus rock,
driving the vulture from his midriff...

So when the Fates decide my time is up,
and I'm just a short name on a scrap of marble,
Maecenas, hope and envy of young Romans,
source of my glory both in life and death,
should your road chance to bring you near my tomb,
pull up your British chariot with carved fittings,
and strew my ash with tears and words like these:
'His ruin was a woman's cruelties.'

II.2

Free at last, I had thought of having my bed to myself,
but Amor, after striking a peace-deal, double-crossed me...
Why is a face like that *allowed* to exist on earth?
Jupiter, I'll overlook your conquests of old.

Her hair's tawny, her fingers long; she walks tall
using her whole body, a worthy sister for Jove,
or like Minerva striding to the altars of Athens,
the Gorgon's serpentine locks upon her breastplate.

Give up, you goddesses shepherd Paris watched
lowering your underwear on Ida's peaks.
May age refuse to change her face, even if
she lives the centuries of the Sibyl of Cuma.

II.3

'You said no woman can affect you now.
Wrong! Your arrogance fell at the first hurdle.
You take a break for barely one month and
another book's about to spread scandal about you.'

I was wondering whether a fish might survive on dry sand,
or a wild boar, perhaps, out at sea,
or whether I might burn the candle for serious study:
you can put off love, never get rid of it.

It was less her face that snared me, for all its beauty
(lilies are not whiter than m'lady),
or her hair fashionably floating down her smooth neck,
or the fire in her eyes, my twin lodestars,
or her breasts gleaming through Arabian silk
(call me a flattering lover, but there's some reason) –
than the graceful way she dances when the wine's served,
like Ariadne leading the whooping chorus,
and how she launches into songs like Sappho,
her skill on the lyre a match for the Muses,
and when she compares her writings to those of Corinna
and thinks Erinna's poems inferior.

In the first days after you were born, my darling,
a propitious love-god signalled a good omen.
Divinities gave you gifts from heaven –
don't imagine that you got them from your mother.
Mortal women could not produce such qualities,
even after nine months …
You were born to bring unique glory to the girls of Rome;
so perhaps you'll not be content with us human partners,
and become the first Roman to bed Jupiter …

Helen's beauty visits Earth a second time.
Should I be surprised if our young men are hot for her?
She would have been a finer cause for Troy's ruin.
I used to marvel how a woman had started
such a war between Europe and Asia at Pergamum.
No one could fault you, Menelaus, or you, Paris,
the one for demanding her back, the other for stalling.

This was the face that Achilles worthily died for;
even Priam approved it as the *casus belli*.

Anyone with ambitions to outstrip the old masters
should make my true love his model in his painting:
wherever he exhibits her in the world,
East or West, he will set it on fire.

II.4

A girlfriend, you say?
Accept you'll have manifold sins to complain of;
you'll make a pitch often, as often be repulsed,
your poor fingernails ruined by toothmarks,
the irregular tap of your feet in irritation...

I myself once plastered my hair
with gel (what a waste of time),
walked that slow, studied walk ...

It's no case for herbal remedies, moonlight magic,
grasses stewed by Medea or Perimede.
We don't know the causes or see the blows coming –
where this shower of troubles starts is a mystery.
The patient needs no doctors or comfortable beds;
it's not the season or weather that's bothering him.
He goes for a walk – the next minute
his friends are escorting his hearse:
love's an unpredictable matter
(whatever love is).
Yet I keep every swindling fortune-teller in business.
Every Gypsy Rose has gone through my dreams ten times...

I wish my enemies the love of women;
and all my friends the pleasures of a boy –
a safe boat to punt down a gentle river:
what harm can come from such a little stream?
One word can often mollify a boy:
a woman won't be satisfied with your blood.

II.5

Is it reasonable, Cynthia, that
you gallivant around Rome,
leading a life of public disrepute?

Have I deserved this? You'll pay
for your disloyalty –
the wind can blow me too in another direction.

There are hordes of deceitful women
out there, but I shall find one
who'll appreciate being famous through my poems,

not humiliate me with
outrageous behaviour, but prick you
with memories of my long love, your belated tears.

While I'm still in a fury,
now's time for me to part:
if there's no pain, love will always creep back.

The swell of Aegean waves
does not rise in a north wind
or black clouds scud about in a treacherous southerly

as quickly as angry lovers
change their tune; while you still can,
duck your neck from out that heavy yoke.

It won't hurt at all, or at least
not after the first night:
all love pains are mild, if you just wait them out.

By the sweet laws imposed
by your patron goddess Juno,
stop hurting me with your spite, my darling:

It's not just a bull that strikes
an enemy with its horns –
even a wounded sheep fights its attacker.

I'm not going to tear the clothes
from off your faithless body,
my anger won't break down your bolted doors,

nor shall I pull out your plaited
hair in a fit of rage
or dig my fingers into you to hurt you.

I'll leave that unbecoming
retaliation to some peasant,
it's not for a poet wreathed in an ivy garland.

No, I'll write something that can't be
erased for the rest of your life:
'Cynthia so lovely and such an easy lay.'

You may have nothing but scorn
for gossip, but believe me,
that will cause your cheeks to pale, my Cynthia.

II.6

No similar crowd besieged the house of Lais,
though all Greece was prostrate outside;
nor did such numbers once mob Thais,
who kept the men of Athens satisfied;
and Phryne, who could have rebuilt Thebes' ruins,
never pocketed so many contributions.
You even invent imaginary male relations
to ensure a supply of those you can decently kiss.

Pictures of young men upset me, even their names,
a baby boy in a cradle who can't even blabber.
It upsets me if your sister or mother
kisses you, or a girlfriend shares your bedroom.
Everything upsets me: insecurity – pay no heed!
I see a skirt: I think there's a man inside.

Sex. In the past it led to wars,
was at the root of the carnage at Troy;
the same insanity made the Centaurs
smash their sharp-edged cups against Pirithous.
But why look for Greek examples? Romulus,
fed on harsh she-wolf milk, gave instruction in crime:
how to rape the Sabine virgins and get away;
thanks to him Amor now runs riot in Rome.
What point in building temples of Chastity
if brides simply go wherever they please?
I bless the wives of Admetus and Ulysses,
any woman who prefers her husband's home.

Whoever started painting rude pictures,
decorating respectable homes with indecent scenes,
corrupted the innocent eyes of girls,
wanting them to share his depravity.

May he moan in hell, the man who used those skills
to disclose rites hidden in silent ecstasy!
Houses were never adorned in times past with those figures:
you wouldn't find crimes plastered on the walls.
Now the spider has wrapped undeserving shrines,
grass overgrows unjustly abandoned deities.

Do I put guards on you, bar your door,
so no enemy foot may pass through?
Surveillance is futile if the will's not there;
being ashamed to cheat on me, Cynthia,
would be security enough for you.

II.7

You must have celebrated, Cynthia:
they pulled the law we had long dreaded
would split us up (though even Jupiter
can't part lovers against their will).
Caesar is great, but great in war:
defeated tribes don't count in love.

No wife or girlfriend will divide
us – you'll always be both for me.
I'd frankly rather be beheaded
than waste good torches on a bride,
or, as a groom, pass your closed door,
lamenting what I had betrayed.
Worse than a funeral dirge, that wedding march
would ruin, darling, your sweet sleep!
Breed sons for national victory?
No soldier's coming from my blood.

But for a legionnaire in Cynthia's army,
Castor's great horse would not suffice.
You're why they read my poetry
even beside the Dnieper's winter ice.
It's you alone I want to please and keep:
that's more to me than fatherhood.

II.8

My long-time lover is snatched away
and you tell me to keep a stiff upper lip, my friend?
There's a unique nastiness to love quarrels:
garotte me and my rage might abate.
Can I watch her lie in the crook of another man's arm?
They said she was mine and now they'll say she's not?
Great leaders, great dictators have often fallen;
Thebes and towering Troy – they're history.

So you'll die in the flush of youth, Propertius;
die then, make her happy!
She can bother my ghost, chase after my shade,
dance on my pyre, trample my bones!
Didn't Haemon fall on Antigone's tomb,
stabbing himself with his own sword?
Didn't he mix his bones with hers,
rather than go home without her?
Don't think you'll escape: you'll have to die with me;
the blood of both of us dripping from one blade,
shameful as that death will be to me;
shameful maybe – but you'll die.

Achilles, when his woman was taken away,
hung up his weapons, alone in his tent.

He'd seen the Greek rout, the bodies on the shore,
Hector's torches, the Greek camp swarming like ants;
Patroclus disfigured, smeared with sand,
lying dead, tangle-haired;
he sat through it all because of beautiful Briseis,
such pain boiled in him for his stolen love.
When the captive was returned, belated amends made,
he dragged the mighty Hector behind his horses.
I don't have Achilles' mother or his armour –
what's to wonder at if love triumphs over me?

II.9

What he is, I've been often; but perhaps in an hour
he'll be out as well and another will be in.

Penelope managed to see out twenty years
on her own, though such a catch for suitors,
remarriage put off by a pretence of weaving,
her day's work furtively by night unravelled;
she'd see Ulysses again, scarcely believing
she would, and grown old waiting on his travels.

Briseis, hugging Achilles' lifeless body,
pummelled her lovely face with maddened hands;
the weeping captive washed her bloodied
lord laid out on Simois' yellow sand,
then, holding his great bones in her small palms,
Achilles' corpse cremated, soiled her hair.

Greece boasted loyal brides in ancient times:
honour prevailed amid carnage and war.

You did not last one night without a partner
or pass a solitary morning, faithless hussy.
What if I were a soldier in the far
East Indies, or my ship becalmed at sea?
You knocked back the wine and laughed out loud;
no doubt I figured in your malicious talk.
You even chase a man who once walked out.
Let's hope you make it with him, and good luck!
When Styx's waters swirled around your head,
was it for this I prayed you would recover
and stood with weeping friends beside your bed?
What sign then, madam, of your latest lover?

Not hard for you to spin deceptive tales:
it's something women always learned to do.
The leaves don't flutter in a wintry gale
and treacherous Libyan shoals don't shift as soon
as promises collapse under female
anger for reasons serious or no.

The stars are witness and the morning dew,
the door that opened after a night-long wait,
I never loved another more than you,
nor will I now, for all your spite.
No woman will leave imprints on my pillow:
if I cannot be yours I'll stay alone.
And if I've lived life rightly, may that fellow
at love-making's crescendo turn to stone!

II.10

High time for a different dance on the slopes of Helicon,
time to clear the field for the cavalry.
I'd like to report on squadrons itching for combat,
detail The Leader's Roman campaigns.
If my powers fail, I'll get credit certainly
for effort: in a major enterprise
just the aspiration to do it is enough.
'Began with love lyric, later turned to epic.'
I'll sing of war, the girl theme being written out.
I'm perfecting the furrowed brow, the more ponderous step;
my Muse is teaching me a new instrument.

Brain, stop thinking trivial verse; flex
your muscles, Muses; the deep voice is needed now.
The Euphrates is saying no more cover for
the Parthian horsemen's rear-guard;
it's sorry it stopped the Crassi going home.
Even India, Augustus, is stretching out
its neck for your yoke; the virgin land
of Arabia trembles before you;
and any country cowering at the world's end
is going to feel your conquering hand hereafter.
That's the camp I'll follow; hymning your campaigns
will make me a great bard (I hope I live to see it).

When you can't reach a statue's head to place a garland,
lay it beneath its feet;
I can't – at the moment – scale the heights of glory,
so offer cheap incense in a poor man's rites.
My poems have not yet climbed Hesiod's mountain,
but are washed in the valley stream by Love.

II.11

Let others write about you, or you will be unknown:
    let him praise you who sows in sterile ground.
The black day, believe me, will carry off all your gifts
    along with you on one funeral bier;
and the traveller will ignore your remains as he goes past,
    not saying: 'This ash was once a cultured girl.'

II.12

Amazing hands, don't you think,
whoever first painted love as a child?
He saw that lovers live irrational lives,
trivial concerns eclipse the greater good.

He pointedly added wings for a quick getaway
when the god takes off from the human heart;
we are tossed about from one wave to the next:
our breeze doesn't keep to any quarter.

And rightly his hand is armed with barbed arrows,
a quiver slung across both shoulders –
he takes us out before we spot the enemy,
no chance of escaping unscathed.

In me his shafts remain – and his childish image;
but certainly he's lost his wings,
for he's flying nowhere from my chest,
waging endless war within my veins.

What kicks do you get, boy, living in dried-out bones?
Shame on you, take your weapons some other place.

Better try your poison on those yet to taste it;
I'm not being thrashed, just my flimsy shadow.

Lose me, and who'll sing of you then
(my Muse's light touch brought you great renown),
or the head and fingers of my dark-eyed love
and how softly, when she walks, her feet move?

II.13

All the arrows in Persia
are less than the darts Amor
has fixed in my chest. He's banned me
from spurning the slender Muses,
ordered me to live in the grove of Helicon;
not so I might make oaks
listen to my words or play
pied piper to wild animals,
rather that Cynthia might be
bewitched by my verse: then my art
would outstrip the fame of Linus.

It's not so much I admire
good looks or a woman who boasts
famous ancestry; what I like
is reciting my poems in the lap
of a well-read girl and having
her delicate ear approve them.
If so, what do I care
for the babble of the crowd,
safe in my true-love's judgment?
If she'll listen favourably
to my peace offering, I
can tolerate even Jupiter's ill-will.

So when death shuts my eyes,
here are my funeral directions:
no long line of family images in my cortege,
no vain trumpet lament for my fate,
no ivory stand for my coffin,
no gold-braided sheet for my body,
no row of scent-bearing dishes.
What *do* I want?
The small observances of a plebeian funeral.

I'll be happy to take three slim volumes
as a special gift for Persephone.
You'll be following, baring and tearing
your breast, you'll never tire
of calling out my name,
planting last kisses on
my cold lips, as a jar
of Syrian unguent is offered.

Then when fire has reduced
me to ashes, a little urn
can hold my remains, a bay shrub
placed over my humble tomb
to shade the site of my burnt-out
pyre, and a two-line inscription:
WHO LIES HERE NOW, STARK DUST,
WAS SERVANT OF JUST ONE LOVE.

My grave will be no less famous
than the bloody tomb of Achilles.
When you feel your own end coming,
remember to visit, white-haired,
once again these memorial stones.
Meanwhile, don't spurn me in death –
the earth can divine the truth.

One of the sister Fates
should have ordered me to surrender
my soul as I slept in my cradle.
Why preserve the breath
of a life that's so uncertain?
Nestor lived three generations.
Had a Trojan soldier cut short
his old age on the Greek earthworks,
he'd never have seen Antilochus'
body interred or said:
'Death, why do you come so late?'

You'll sometimes weep for your lost
lover: it's right to always
love men who have gone before.
A wild boar killed the fair
Adonis hunting in Cyprus;
Venus washed his beautiful
body in the marsh pool, they say,
and wandered, her hair unkempt.
Cynthia, you'll call in vain
to my silent ghost to return:
what can my crumbled bones reply to you?

II.14

Happiness was: Agamemnon when he won
the Trojan War, pocketing that city's wealth;
Ulysses when his wanderings were done
and his keel touched the sand of Ithaca;
Electra seeing Orestes was not dead,
having mourned her brother's supposed remains;
Ariadne finding Theseus unharmed,
led from the labyrinth by her ball of thread.

My pleasures last night exceeded those by far:
one more like it and I shall be immortal.

I once went pleading to her with bowed head,
only to hear her say I was cheap as dirt.
Now her fastidiousness is no obstacle,
she can't sit there, unmoved by my entreaties.
My one regret – I learned the trick so late,
like medicine to make a corpse feel well.
The path was clear: I was too blind to see it.
(No one sees anything when they're lovelorn.)
What I grasped was this: lovers must show *scorn*.
Yesterday she was 'busy'; today she'll come.

Rivals pounded her door, called her their 'lady-love';
she ignored them, her head snuggled against me.
Victory over the Parthians? Small potatoes!
Here are my spoils, my captured kings, my chariot.
Venus, I'm nailing my offerings to your temple,
and underneath some rhyme like this:

PROPERTIUS LAYS THESE GIFTS BEFORE YOUR SHRINE
IN THANKS FOR ONE WHOLE NIGHT WHEN SHE WAS MINE.

It's your decision, darling, whether my boat
comes safe to port or founders in the shallows.
If any offence by me should change your mind,
find me at your doorway – lying lifeless.

II.15

Yes!
A night to circle on the calendar!
Even the bed enjoyed my darling's body!
She kissed my eyes open when they drooped in sleep:
'Just lying there, you slacker?'
We explored every embrace, those kisses
refusing to fade on my lips.
We talked and talked with the lamp pulled close,
but what a tussle when the light was dimmed!
At times she bared her breasts to grapple with me,
then hid them behind her night-shirt to slow down.

It spoils the fun to cuddle in the dark.
Eyes are love-leaders, as I think you know.
Paris, they say, was entranced seeing Helen
naked, when she slipped from her husband's room.
Naked, Endymion captivated the moon goddess,
naked slept with her, the story goes.
But if you insist on going to bed in clothes,
your dress might just get torn by my rough hand.
I might just get carried away and leave
bruises on your arms to show your mother!
Boobs sloping earthward need not spoil the game:
no call for *post partum* embarrassment.
Life's short, let's glut our eyes with love:
a long night's coming for you, with no dawn.

If only you would want us chained so tightly
no day could ever part us,
doves in the bond of passion,
male and female, total union.
He's wrong who seeks a limit to love's madness.
Real love can know no bounds:

farmers will sooner sow one crop and reap
another, the sun drive horses of darkness,
and rivers suck their waters back to their sources,
the fish stranded on the dried-out beds,
than I will take my fires elsewhere:
I'll be one woman's in life, in death also.

If sometimes she will give me nights like these,
a year will be eternity.
Let everybody lead a life like mine,
stretching out their limbs with copious wine –
then there would be no cruel steel or warships,
the sea of Actium would not churn our bones,
and Rome would not so often dress in mourning
to wearily mark its self-imposed defeats.
Generations to come will praise me, justly –
no gods were offended by our carousing.

While the light holds, don't spurn life's fruit, my darling:
all the kisses you can give me will be too few,
and as the petals fall from withering
garlands and you see them float in bowls,
so today we breathe love to the full,
but tomorrow may be our day of reckoning.

II.16a

The governor's home from the Balkans, Cynthia –
huge pickings for you, huge concern for me.
Couldn't he have drowned on the reefs of Albania?
Neptune, what gifts I would have showered you with!
As it is (in my absence) the tables will groan at the parties;
as it is (in my absence) the door will stand wide all night long.

If you'll take my advice, reap the harvest you're offered,
shear the dumb sheep with the long, silky fleece.
Then when his gifts are all gone and he's out of cash,
tell him to find a ship back to some other province.
But, Venus, do me a favour to ease my troubles:
just let him break his balls with his constant screwing.

II.16b

Anyone can buy her love with presents, then.
Lord, the girl goes down for a shameful price!
Cynthia has no interest in titles or medals:
size matters for her in lovers (pocket size).
She's always sending me overseas for jewels,
to bring her gifts from Tyre itself.

I wish there were no rich men in Rome
and even The Leader lived in a thatched cottage.
Girlfriends could never be purchased then for goods,
they'd simply grow old in the houses they were born in.
Never then would you sleep seven nights away from me,
your pretty arms round some repellent man;
a slave sans loin-cloth goes through his paces at market,
then is suddenly rich and the master of my kingdom –
not for anything I've done wrong (I swear) but because
beauty commonly comes with inconstancy.

Will no outrage of yours ever make me cut my losses?
Must it be the same cycle – you misbehave and I hurt?
For *days* now I have felt no interest in
the theatre or gym. Even poetry's no help.
I should be ashamed of course, unless, as they say,
a worthless love is deaf …

Remember the leader who filled Actium Bay
with sound and fury (and with his doomed servicemen):
his sordid love made him turn his ships around
and flee to the furthest corner of the globe.

Whatever clothes, whatever emeralds
or topazes flashing yellow he's given you,
let me see the storm winds carry them into space,
leaving you just their elements – earth and water.
Presents! – Look what they brought Eriphyla,
and the agony in which Creusa burned!

Jupiter's not always soft on perjured lovers
or deaf to prayers for their comeuppance.
You've seen the thunder roll around the sky,
the lightning bolts leap down.
It's not the Pleiades, not Orion doing it,
the lightning's anger isn't over nothing.
He's usually punishing unfaithful girls,
the god who himself has been deceived and wept.

Don't covet a dress from Sidon so much that
you panic whenever the south wind whips up clouds.

II.17

To welsh on a promised night,
to lead on your lover, is
to stain your hands with his blood.

I am the bard of these things:
many loveless nights

spent on my own, broken
by our beds' separation.

Pity Tantalus at
the river, the water cheating
his thirst, parching his mouth.
Watch Sisyphus rolling
the elusive boulder uphill.

But nothing is worse on
this earth than the lover's life,
nobody you'd less wish
to be if you had any sense.

I, whose good fortune once
brought tears to the goddess Envy,
now enter my girl's house
barely one day in ten.
No more cuddles at
the crossroads *au clair de la lune*,
or sliding *billets doux*
under her door. So be it.
I'm not changing my beloved.

She'll be sorry when she sees my loyalty.

II.18

Endless complaining alienates many people:
women often fall for the silent type.
If you saw something, always deny you saw it;
if something really hurt, shrug it off.

Suppose the years were turning my hair white,
creeping wrinkles furrowing my cheeks?
Dawn did not despise Tithonus when he aged
or let him lie alone in their eastern home.
She chided the gods when she climbed into her chariot
and did her job reluctantly for Earth.
When she came home she often gave him a warm bath
even before she'd scrubbed down her unharnessed horses.
She embraced him going to bed over there near India,
and lamented that daytime was coming round too soon.
Her joy in Tithonus as he grew elderly
was greater than her grief at the loss of Memnon.
That girl was not embarrassed to sleep with an old man
and smother his white hair with kisses.

I'm still a young man, yet you're so disloyal you hate me,
though you'll be a bent old woman yourself before long.

II.19

I'm sorry, Cynthia, you're deserting Rome,
but I'm relieved you'll be alone in the country.
No young Don Juans prowl the virtuous fields
to try your virtue with their artistry;
no brawls will break out beneath your windows,
no one disrupt your sleep, calling your name.
You'll be on your own, Cynthia, with mountains to look at,
sheep, and the peasants' fields. There'll be no shows
to fray your moral fibre, no temples (it is there
you often start to misbehave). You can watch
the oxen plough up and down, the vine-shoots
pruned with slender sickles. You'll burn incense
as a young goat is slaughtered at a rustic altar.

And with your dress hitched up you'll dance;
but safe from intruders, safe from the male kind.

For my part, I'll go hunting, take a break
from Venus, observe the rites of Diana instead.
I'll get the baying hounds on the move, I'll slay
wild creatures, hang their antlers on the pines;
I'm not quite ready, yet, for great big lions
or grappling hand-to-hand with wild boar:
I might be brave enough to bag a furry hare
or two, snare birds with quicklimed twigs,
where Clitunno streams through the shade
of an elegant grove, its waters washing cattle
snowy. Any fun and games, sweetheart,
from you, remember, I'll be coming
to get you in a few days. The lonely woods,
the streams meandering down mossy ridges won't
stop me worrying that your name
might come to me on someone else's tongue –
taking advantage of an absent lover?

II.20

From the way you cry,
one would think you were worse off than abducted Briseis,
more desperate than captured Andromache;
bothering the gods ranting about my 'deceit'
and whining that all my promises 'ended like this'.
You outdo the mourning dove in the leaves of Athens;
even Niobe, whose boasting slew her twelve progeny,
didn't weep such waterfalls from the mountain.

They can tie me down with bronze fetters,
lock you up in the dungeon of Danae –
I'll break those chains to reach you, darling,
burst into that steel-plated chamber.
Any rumours that reach me about you fall on deaf ears:
so don't *you* be in any doubt about *my* seriousness.
I swear by the memory of my mother and father
(may their ashes crush me if I lie)
that I will stay yours till that last nightfall:
one commitment, one day that will take us both.

If it weren't your name or your beauty that kept me constant,
it would be the easy terms of serving you.
Six moons have waxed and waned
since we became the talk of each street corner –
and still your door swings open on its hinges,
still there's the cornucopia of your bed.
Not a single night have I bought with lavish gifts:
for everything I thank your generous soul.
Many wanted you, but you single-mindedly
chose me: how could I now forget your love?
If I did, then harry me, Furies of tragedy;
condemn me, Aeacus, in the judgement of hell;
let me lie amid Tityus' flock of vultures,
push rocks uphill like Sisyphus …

No need to bombard me, then, with plaintive letters:
my faith will be to the end what it was on day one.

II.21

May Venus curse Panthus on a scale that matches
the enormity of the lies he's spread about me!

I'm a better prophet, it seems, than Dodona's oracle:
that pretty-boy lover of yours has acquired a wife, sweetheart.
All those nights of passion wasted. Galling, isn't it?
He's whistling, shot of you. You were too credulous.
Now you're alone in bed.

The happy couple will be talking about you; the arrogant
bastard will say you used to gate-crash his home.
Let's face it: the only value you have for him
is a notch on his bedpost, a trophy of bachelor days.
He deceived you as Jason did his Colchian hostess:
she was kicked out as soon as Creusa grabbed him.
He gave you the slip as Ulysses did Calypso:
all she saw was her lover spreading sail.

Some girls are just too inclined to take things at face-value;
they should learn when abandoned – kindness can be
                                        misplaced.
What now? For some time you've been hunting another man.
Once bitten, best to be shy, you idiot:
meanwhile, any time, any place, I'm going to be
available, 'in sickness and in health'.

II.22a

Recently I've fancied many girls equally,
as you know, Demophoon; and, as you also know,
big trouble results.

There's no street corner I pass without consequences,
while the theatre was clearly invented for my ruin.
A lady spreading her pretty arms on stage
with a sultry look, perhaps, or singing an aria.
My eyes actively look for irritations:
a blonde in the audience with revealing cleavage,
stray hair wandering down a smooth forehead,
a jewel in the middle, Indian-style …
And why, you ask, Demophoon, am I so very
susceptible to them all?
There is no 'why' in love's vocabulary.
Why do people cut their arms with knives
in religious dances to some Phrygian tune?
We all get from nature some vice when our lives begin:
mine happens to be constantly falling in love.
Even if I suffer the fate of Thamyras the singer,
I'll never be blind, jealous friend, to gorgeous women.

II.22b

Sometimes the sun, sometimes the moon lights the sky,
you'll have noticed.
Ditto with me: one girlfriend is one too few.
Girl B can fondle me with eager arms
if Girl A decides she can't fit me in;
if one gets cross with one of my messages,
she should be aware there's another who wants to say yes.

Two's such a good number: two cables secure a ship,
a mother's less anxious with twins than an only child.

If you think all this is making me thin and wasted,
you're wrong: the worship of Venus is labour-saving.

Just ask around: many girls know from experience
mine is an all-night service.
For Alcmena's benefit, Jupiter stopped in their tracks
other heavenly bodies …
The sky did without the boss for two nights running,
but he wasn't too tired to hurl a few thunderbolts afterwards.
Love doesn't deplete the energy it will need.

When Achilles tore himself from Briseis' embrace,
were the Trojans less inclined to run from the Greeks?
Conversely, when Hector rose from Andromache's bed,
did the Greek fleet have nothing to fear from combat?
The Greeks stood to lose their ships, the Trojans their walls:
I am Achilles in love, fierce Hector am I.

II.23-24a

I shunned the highway of the ignorant mob
only to drink now from the public taps.
What free man bribes some servant for the job
of taking messages to his girlfriend's steps?
Or forever asks in what porticoes she's
walking now, in which park he should have sought her;
carries out the labours of Hercules,
only to have her ask what gift he's bought her?
To see the ugly mug of some foul guard,
get caught and locked up in a squalid hut?
For one night's joy per year the work is hard!
I can't bear girls who keep their front doors shut.
Give me the one whose charms are on display
with coat thrown back – no fear of any goon.
Her shabby shoes wear down the Sacred Way:
come close, no waiting, she delivers soon!
No likelihood she'll wheedle to receive

presents your father will complain about,
or tell you: 'Quick! It's time for you to leave.
My husband's back in town today. Get out!'
The flotsam of the Orontes and Euphrates
for me, not raiding marriage beds. He's free
whose amorous taste extends to low-cost ladies;
clandestine love puts paid to liberty.

'How can you say that when your Cynthia met
such fame and your book's read in every place?'
Those words should make me break out in cold sweat:
gentlemen hide their love or risk disgrace.
If Cynthia only showed herself more willing,
I wouldn't be the world's most dissolute rake,
or branded round this city as a villain;
I'd burn without illusions for her sake.
Don't marvel if I favour girls-for-sale:
they bring less scandal. Isn't that good reason?
She wants a fan from some proud peacock's tail,
glass balls to cool her hands in the hot season.
When cross she asks me for those ivory dice,
trinkets the Sacred Way would have you acquire.
Though I don't give a toss about the price,
being conned by a cheating girl – that cost is higher.

II.24b

This is it, then, the bliss you promised me?
'So beautiful – and so fickle.' Aren't you ashamed?
Barely one or two nights of love and already
it turns out I'm a threat to your bed-springs.
A short while back you were praising me, reading my poems;
a quick flash of wings and Amor changes direction?

Let this man compete with my talent, my writings;
and first, let him learn his roving days are over.
If you like, let him fight the Hydra of Lerna,
bring you apples snatched from the Hesperides' snake;
maybe swallow vile poisons, the salt water of shipwreck,
never shirk any misery for your sake.
(I wish, darling, you'd put me through those tests).
This tiger will prove to be a pussy-cat,
however much his boasts have pumped up his fame:
you'll break up next year would be my forecast.
But I won't be changed by the Sibyl's longevity,
or the labours of Hercules or death's black day.

You'll lay me out, saying: 'Propertius, are these
your bones? You loved me till your last hour,
you were loyal, although no blue-blooded
aristocrat, and certainly not that rich.'
I'll tolerate anything; treat me badly – it makes
no difference: a beautiful woman's a light burden.
Beauty – many men, I think, fell for that,
but not many had, I think, the staying power.
Theseus' love for Ariadne was short-lived,
and Demophoon's for Phyllis, two bad guests.
Medea, famously taken on Jason's ship,
was abandoned by the man she had just saved.

Don't offer yourself to men of high birth or money:
they won't be at your funeral when that day arrives.
But I will be – though I pray you'll be mourning me,
unfastening your hair, beating your bare breasts.

II.25

Cynthia, most lovely obsession,
               born to hurt me,
(locked doors were ever my fate),
my slim volumes will make your beauty sweep the world,
by leave of Calvus
          & *pace* Catullus.
The veteran takes off his weapons,
               goes into retirement,
in old age bulls refuse to pull the plough,
the crumbling ship rests on empty sand,
the worn-out shield
               lies unused in some temple.
However old I get,
          I won't stop loving you even
if I'm a latter-day Tithonus or Nestor.

Better, surely, to have served a ruthless tyrant
               & groaned in cruel Perillus' bull?
Better to have turned to stone at the Gorgon's stare,
          even been chewed by those Caucasus vultures?
I'll stick with it, though.
Rust wears down the iron sword
          & water droplets flint.
But the drip-drip of his girl's recriminations
               never wears down the lover:
his undeserving ear outlasts her anger.
Spurn him, he keeps on asking,
          confesses he's wrong
even when right, comes back for more
               on reluctant feet.

You, my friend, who put on airs
          because your love's at its zenith,

don't be fooled: long-term constancy
        is not something women are known for.
Who discharges vows to the gods as the storm is raging,
when ships can get torn to splinters
                        even in port?
What charioteer claims his prize with the race still on,
        before his axle goes down the home straight?
In love, mendacious winds pretend to favour us:
when disaster strikes late
                        it strikes hardest.

Meanwhile, though she says she loves you,
        keep that good feeling to your chest, eh?
She may call you often – you just need to go once:
what arouses envy
                often is short-lived.
If today's girls were enamoured of the old ways,
I'd be where you are now:
                        time defeats me.
Not that the new ways will change my character:
        each to his own path.

You men who scout for multiple love-affairs,
that way lies painful torture of the eyes!
You see a girl with soft, pure white skin,
& you see a dark one;
                each complexion entices.
You see Greek girls walking the way they do,
& you see Roman girls;
                        each figure captivates.
One dresses casually,
        one in *haute couture*:
no matter – all roads lead to doom.

Just one woman's eyes spell I-N-S-O-M-N-I-A,

so one woman's enough;
              lots of them's bad news.

II. 26a

I dreamed I saw you shipwrecked, darling,
your hands flailing in the Ionian Sea,
and you confessing all the lies you'd told me,
though you couldn't even lift your soaking hair.
Thinking of Helle, tossed by purple waves
when she fell from the soft back of the golden sheep,
I feared you might name a sea – the Cynthiaspont! –
and sailors, gliding through your strait, would weep.
The prayers I raised to Neptune, Castor, Pollux
(and Helle's deified stepmother too)!

And now your hands just reach above the swirl;
you're going to die, you keep calling my name.
If Glaucus saw your eyes you'd be his girl
of the Ionian Sea,
with nymphs muttering enviously about you,
white Nesaee, cerulean Cymothoe ...

But then I saw a dolphin race to save you,
surely the one that carried Arion and his lyre.
I was thinking of diving down from off a rock,
when my dream vanished and I woke from shock.

II.26b

My girl is thinking of making
a long sea journey. I'll go with her,
one wind blowing two lovers,
one beach where we'll sleep,
one tree for our cover,
one spring for us to drink,
one plank where we both can lie,
whether prow or stern is our bunk.

Nothing will be too hard for me,
though a vicious east wind harasses
or a cold southerly drives our sails
towards the uncertain, the gales
that tormented Ulysses
and the thousand ships of the Greeks
on the Evia coast, or moved two rocks
when a dove was sent to guide
the Argo's maiden voyage
over an unknown sea.
So long as I can see her,
Jove himself can burn our vessel.
We'll be flung naked together
on the same shore: let the water
sweep me away, provided
the earth will give you burial.

But Neptune won't be hard
on a love like ours; as a lover
he matches his brother Jupiter.
Amymone, spread-eagled
in the fields while fetching water
can testify to that, and Lerna
marsh struck by the trident.

The god made good on his promise,
once disentangled from her;
her golden pitcher poured
the water he had conjured.

And ravished Orithyia
will not say the North Wind was cruel,
he who tames the land and the tall seas.
Believe me, even Scylla
will grow gentle, and Charybdis,
whose vast ebb and flow never ceases.
The stars will be unclouded,
Orion clear – and Auriga.

To lay down my life for your body:
a worthy end for us both?

II.27

You seek the unknowable, mortals – your final hour
and the way death will come;
you seek gypsy lore in a clear sky,
what star bodes well or ill for men.

If we march to the Middle East, or sail to Britain,
the dangers of land and sea are in our blind-spot;
at home, revolution has us in its sights,
its outcome wavering as forces join battle;
houses go up in flames or down in ruins,
dark potions await your lips.

Only the lover knows when he will perish
and why; he fears no weaponry or north wind.

Though he sits in the Stygian reed-beds, oar in hand,
and sees the deadly sails of the underworld ferry:
should the distant call of his girl come wafting down,
he'll make the forbidden journey back to the living.

II.28

Jupiter, *miserere* this sick girl:
if such beauty dies, you will bear the guilt.
Comes the season of wavering heat haze,
the dry earth starts to bake in the dog days –
but the weather's not to blame, nor the crimes of heaven,
so much as disrespecting the gods so often.

Is Venus piqued they compared you to her? That goddess
always was resentful of loveliness.
Did you neglect the temples of Juno,
or say Minerva's eyes were … well … so-so?
You beauties can be careless in your language.
Your looks have caused it, and your sharp tongue.
After all the perils, though, of a troubled life
may your last day bring time of relief.

For ages Io, head down, was a lowing cow
and drank from the Nile, where she's worshipped now.
Ino, who roamed the earth in earlier years,
is the recipient of sailors' prayers.
Callisto paced Arcadia as a bear:
now ships at night are guided by her star.

Should fate bring forward your *requiem
aeternam*, beatified by burial, then
you'll tell Semele of beauty's dangers;

she'll believe it, taught by her own misadventures;
among all Homer's heroines you'll be
in first place; none of them will not make way.
As best you can, submit to fate in sickness:
the gods can change; so can *illa dies*.

The magician's wand and chant prove of no worth,
the laurel lies scorched in the burnt-out hearth,
the moon's had it with falling from the sky,
the owl hoots death's litany.
A single ship of fate will take
our love, dark sails spread on the infernal lake.
Miserere, I pray, not one but two:
if she lives, I live; if she falls, I do.

Grant my pleas and I'll commit to sacred verse:
I'll write: MY GIRL SAVED BY GREAT JUPITER;
and, reverently sitting at your feet, she'll
tell you the story of her long ordeal.
Your wife Juno will allow you this:
she's diminished too by any girl's demise.
Persephone, stay clement; and her spouse,
Pluto, be no more malicious.

So many beautiful women are there below;
let one remain up here, if it may be so.
Europa is with you and sinful Pasiphae,
and all the finest of old Crete and Achaia,
Thebes and the kingdom of Priam, fallen in ruin;
you have Antiope, Tyro of the fair skin,
and every Roman woman in beauty's roll-call
has died; the gluttonous pyre consumed them all.

Light of my life, released now from great danger,
pay Diana her due gift, dance for her;

perform vigils for her who was bovine, now divine.

And perform for me – ten votive nights are mine.

II.29a

I was roaming the streets, plastered, last night, darling –
I'd given the servants the evening off –
when a gang of diminutive youths waylaid me
(in my fright, I forgot to count them);
some were grasping torches, others arrows,
and some even looked about to tie me up.
Anyway, they were naked. The boldest of them
said: 'Grab him. You know who he is.
It's the one that angry woman hired us to get.'

He'd hardly said this and a rope was round my neck.
One called for me to be pushed forward; another
said: 'Let's do him in – he doesn't believe we're gods.
As for you, you jerk, she's been waiting up for you
till all hours: you don't deserve her; you're on the prowl
for some other woman.
When she takes off her bonnet and lifts her heavy eyes,
what's going to hit you is not the fragrances
of Arabian herbs but those
Amor himself created with his own hands.
Okay, we'll let him off, brothers, he says he'll be true,
and we've reached the house we were told to bring him to.'

They flung my cloak back on me, saying:
'You can go: just learn to stay at home at night.'

II.29b

Morning.
        I went to see if she was lying
alone: just Cynthia was in her bed.
And stunning: she had never seemed
more gorgeous, even in her red negligee,
going to tell Vesta of her dreams
in case they spelled bad news for her – or me.
She looked as though sleep had just set her free,
a study in the power of pure beauty!

'You're up betimes. Come to spy on your friend?'
she asked. 'You think I live my life like you?
I'm no pushover: I'm content with carnal
knowledge of one man – you, or one more true.
No signs, are there, of hollows in the bed,
no traces of a tumble just for two?
Inspect me – yes, all over.
Am I still panting from some recent sin?'

She brushed away the kiss I offered,
jumped up and found her flip-flops on the floor.
For checking her virtue I was shown the door.

I haven't had an easy night since then.

II.30

Where are you off to so fast,
lunatic? There's no escape:
you can run to the quiet Don – Love will hunt you down.
Mount in the air astride Pegasus, strap

Perseus' wings to your feet,
cut the winds with your heels:
Mercury's high road won't help you.
Amor, the arch villain, looms always over the head
of the lover, then sits heavy on his neck.
He's a cruel, unsleeping jailer, who'll never allow
you to look up. Eyes to the ground, prisoner!

Yet if you sin, the god is open to prayers...
Just look sharp about it!

So you're the hard man? Ready to sail the Black Sea,
the lonely Caspian shores?
Sprinkle the family gods
with the blood of vengeance, bring back
fearsome trophies to the ancestral hearth?

Old buffers can complain
of the partying, but we'll keep on
pounding the road we started, darling;
their ears may be full of the dust of ancient law books,
but this is a place for the sound
of the subtle flute, unjustly thrown
to float in the Maeander when
Minerva thought her puffed cheeks made her ugly.

What's to apologise for
if I'm happy with one woman?
If that's a crime, Amor's the criminal –
don't blame me. Let our pleasure, Cynthia, be
the dews and caverns of the lichenous ridges
where you'll see Muses dotted among the boulders,
singing of the old honey traps for Jupiter,
burned by Semele, undone by Io,
flying at last, an eagle, to Troy's roofs.

If no one's fought Cupid and lived to tell the tale,
why am I alone in the dock for collective guilt?

You won't make the Muses blush:
they know what it is to love;
one, anyway, fell for handsome Oeagrus
and snuggled up with him in the rocks of Thrace.
When they put you at the front of their chorus line,
Bacchus in the middle with his baton,
I'll let the ivy fronds swing from my head:
without you all my inspiration's dead.

II.31–32

Excuse my lateness. The reason? Apollo's gilded
portico was being opened by great Caesar.
It's one big arcade of Saharan stone columns,
interspersed with old Danaus' entire brood of daughters.
Apollo's statue looked finer than the real thing,
the marble mouthing a song to a silent lyre;
Myron's cattle stand around the altar,
four oxen, lifelike signatures of the artist;
in the middle the temple rises in gleaming marble –
the god might prefer it to his native Delos.
Over the pediment the chariot of the sun,
the twin doors a masterpiece of African ivory:
one with the Gauls kicked off Parnassus' summit,
the other lamenting the deaths of Niobe's children.
Apollo himself, between his mother and sister,
plays songs in a long robe ...

You should take a stroll there in your spare time,
Cynthia! But I don't trust you: too many men

have seen you rushing to fulfil your vow
with lit torches at Diana's grove out of town.
And seeing is sinning: only those who don't see you
won't be tempted: eyes are the malefactors.
Why patronise dubious soothsayers in Palestrina,
Cynthia, or visit the walls of Tuscolo?
Why does your carriage take you to Tivoli
so often or down the Appian Way to Lanuvio?
Pompey's portico with its cooling columns
and brocaded hangings is too tacky, is it?
Or the dense row of level-topped plane trees,
or the rivulets spouting from sleeping Maro,
the city filled with the sound of splashing water
suddenly pouring out of Triton's mouth?

I don't think so. Your road's signposted 'Infidelity';
it's not the city you're running from but my scrutiny.
It won't work; your artless schemes against me are pointless;
I know your snares – I've learnt from experience.
But my views scarcely matter; throwing away
your good name will bring you what you deserve, I fear.
A nasty rumour about you reached my ears lately;
it went through the whole city – unpleasant stuff.

But pay no attention to malicious tongues:
gossip was ever the penalty for beauty.
It's not as though you've been caught in possession of
                                        poison;
Apollo will witness that your hands are clean.
A one- (or two-) night stand doesn't bother me –
it's petty crime. Helen, for example,
emigrated after falling for a foreigner,
but was brought back home alive and unpunished.
Venus herself gratified her lust for Mars
but still retained her good standing in heaven.

A goddess loved a shepherd on Mount Ida,
bedding him among the sheep – a goddess, remember;
her sister nymphs calmly watched it all
en masse, as did Silenus and his satyrs;
she'd collected apples with them in the mountain vale,
catching them as they fell into her hand.

In this abundance of fornication, who asked:
'Why is she so rich? Who gave her the money and where
did it come from? Rome is fortunate these days
if only one woman commits moral turpitude'?
Lesbia once did all this and got away with it:
successors will surely attract less opprobrium.
Anyone seeking upholders of old-fashioned virtues
obviously only arrived here yesterday.

Anyone who's managed to dry up the ocean waves,
or pulled down the stars from the sky with his mortal hand,
can think about making our women forswear sin:
the sin-free lifestyle ended with Saturn's reign
and the day flood waters covered the earth;
after the Flood of antiquity, tell me,
who was able to keep their bed undefiled,
when even goddesses slept around with gods?
King Minos' wife once – or so they say –
was seduced by the beauty of a raging bull;
and Danae, for all her bronze prison walls,
couldn't just say no to mighty Jupiter.
So whether you're mimicking Greek or Italian women,
here's my verdict, Cynthia: you're free to go, and good luck!

II.33a

This wretched festival is here again:
Cynthia's on ten nights of abstinence.
Time to abolish the rites Io sent
from the steamy Nile to Italian women.

What goddess so often parts lovers gagging for it?
In all guises, she's been hard on her followers.
Io, your secret affair with Jupiter
led you down many roads across the planet.

When Juno put horns on your woman's head,
changing your speech into a cow's hoarse lowing,
you hurt your mouth so often, chewing
oak leaves and arbutus on your stable bed!

Since Jove stripped away your bestial form,
have you become an arrogant goddess?
Not content with Egypt's swarthy devotees?
Why have you made designs on distant Rome?

What's in it for you if girls sleep alone?
Trust me, you'll get those horns back again,
or else we'll simply ride you out of town:
the Nile and Tiber never did get on.

Cynthia, your piety's brought me to my knees;
once past these nights, we'll compensate:

three times, please.

II.33b

You drink slowly but steadily:
late nights can't stop you.
Your hand's not tired enough to drop those dice.
You're not listening to me,
just letting me prattle on,
as the stars fade.

Death tracked grape fermenting from the start,
the ruin of good water! Icarius
learned the bitter smell of the vine
(those Athenian farmers were right to throttle him).
Centaur Eurytion died of wine,
and the Cyclops – the strong vintage.
Liquor destroys looks,
corrupts youth,
makes a girl unable to tell one lover from another ...

But to you it does nothing, damn it!
Drink on – you're beautiful,
wine won't hurt you.
Your garlands droop into your glass,
you read my poems aloud in a high voice ...
Oh, soak the table some more with spilt Falernian,
let it fizz softly in that gilded cup.

II.34

Who'd trust even their best friend with a lovely
woman? I almost lost my own that way.
My researches prove it: anyone will double-cross
you in love; no man can resist a pretty lady.

Amor breaks up the family, wrecks friendship –
all harmony yesterday, broadswords at dawn today.
Menelaus' guest checked out with his host's spouse;
Medea chased after a man she barely knew.

You scoundrel, how could you touch up
my darling? Didn't your hands drop off, Lynceus?
Suppose she hadn't been so firm and true?
Could you have lived with all that infamy?

Poison me or run cold steel through my chest –
just stay away from my sweetheart, that's all.
You may be committed to me, body and soul,
you can take charge of my financial affairs,
but keep out of my bed's my one request:
I can't brook rivals – even Jupiter.
I'm jealous of my insubstantial shadow,
I shake from fear of nothing. I'm such a fool.

I can forgive your shameful behaviour, though,
on one ground: it must have been the wine talking.
But don't give me that ascetic furrowed brow:
everyone knows how love is a good thing.

Lynceus, you've got late-onset amorous
dementia – but I'm glad you now worship my deities.
Your books of Socratic wisdom cannot save
you anymore, or knowing the universe's ways.
Epimenides' poems are no use –
your old mentor has nothing to say on hopeless love.
You'd do better to emulate scholarly Philitas
or the dreams of trim Callimachus.

Recount the Achelous River's course,
its waters shattered in a battle of love,

and how the Maeander winds through the Turkish plains
so intricately it doesn't know where it is,
the strange tale of Adrastus' talking horse,
who won at Archemorus' funeral games.
Don't get into the fate of Amphiaraus' chariot
or Capaneus' fall that gratified Jove;
and don't compose Aeschylean tragedies:
relax – it's time to dance to a softer beat.

Get out that fine lathe now to hone your verse;
unbend, poet, write of your own feelings,
or you'll go the way of Antimachus and Homer:
my girl has no time for gods, even the greatest.
No bull will submit to the plough's weight
before its horns are caught in a strong lariat,
and you will not endure love's hardships,
however tough you are, before you're tamed.
These women are not looking into matter's origins,
explanations for the moon's eclipse,
the evidence for life beyond the tomb
or whether lightning has specific targets.

Take me, for example. Little of the family fortune
was left to me, no ancestor triumphed in war,
yet at parties I rule over girls of all shapes
and sizes through a talent you put down.
I like to lie in, still sporting last night's garlands,
pierced to the bone by the bowshot of Amor;
the Battle of Actium? Vergil will be on the case,
he's the man to describe Caesar's mighty warships,
as soon as he's done with the campaigns of Aeneas
and the foundations he laid in Italian land.
Give way, you Roman writers, give way, you Greeks,
something bigger than the *Iliad* is in the works.

Vergil, you tell of the precepts of old Hesiod,
what field is best for corn, what slope for grapes;
the song you pluck from your subtle lyre
could have come from Apollo's fingers.
You tell of the well-thumbed pipes of Thyrsis
and Daphnis beneath Galaesus' cool pinewoods,
and how to relieve shepherdesses of their dresses
with ten apples and a baby goat from the udder.

Happy man, who can buy love cheap from a girl with apples;
(mine would turn up her nose if Tityrus himself sang to her).
Happy Corydon trying to steal the virginal
Alexis, the treasure of his farmer master.
He may have laid down his pipe from weariness,
but he's still applauded by the tolerant nymphs.
And no reader is going to spurn his poems,
whether expert in love's arts or a novice.

Varro, the crowning passion of Leucadia,
relaxed in this way from the Golden Fleece;
daring Catullus' verse echoed the song:
his Lesbia's better known than Helen is;
erudite Calvus, in pages like these,
wrote of the death of tragic Quintilia.
And how many wounds for lovely Lycoris' sake
did the dead Gallus wash in the underworld lake.

Praised by Propertius, Cynthia will live on,
if fame will lift me to that pantheon.

BOOK THREE

III.1

Ghosts of Callimachus and Philitas of Kos,
admit me, I request you, to your grove.
I come from a pure spring, the first priest
to put Italian rites to a Greek setting.
Tell me, where was the glen where you refined your song
together? How did you start? What water did you drink?

Goodbye, martial epics that hold Apollo back!
Let my verse run, honed on a fine lathe.
That is how fame will raise me from the ground
and my muse ride in triumph on garlanded horses,
the gods of love beside me in the carriage,
a host of writers trailing in my slipstream.
No use shaking your reins to overtake me –
there is no super-highway to the Muses.

Many will add more praises of Rome to the annals,
recounting how Afghanistan
is the empire's new frontier;
but for peacetime reading, this offering comes down
by an untrodden path from the Sisters' mountain.
Give your poet soft wreaths, daughters of Pegasus:
a crown will sit too hard upon my brow.

What the envious crowd takes away from me in life
fame will repay twice over after I die.
After death, time magnifies all things;
funerals are the portal to renown!

Or who would know how a fir-wood horse brought down a city,
how the rivers of Troy battled with Achilles,
how a chariot dragged Hector's body
three times through the dust?

The sons of Priam, poor Paris in his borrowed armour
would scarcely be heard of in their own home town.
There'd be little talk of you these days, Ilium,
twice captured by the power of Hercules ...

were it not for Homer, recorder of your ruin,
who saw his work grow as the ages passed;
and Rome will praise me in
our grandchildren's generation:
I forecast that day will come when I'm turned to ash.
The tombstone marking my bones shall not be neglected.
It's all arranged. Apollo has approved my prayer.

III.2

That said, back to my song-cycle, to gladden
my girl with the touch of the familiar melody.

Orpheus' lyre froze wild beasts in Thrace
and halted eddying rivers, says the legend;
Cithaeron's stones, it's claimed, slid into place
to form Thebes' walls when Amphion played;
and Galatea, beneath Etna's wild slopes, steered
her foam-flecked horses towards the Cyclops' song:
with Apollo and Bacchus on-side, then, what's so strange
if a crowd of women hangs on my every word?

My house is not held up by marble columns;
it has no ivory ceilings with gilded beams,
or orchards like the Gardens of Babylon,
or grottoes cooled by a private water supply;
but my friends are Muses, readers love my poems,
and Calliope dances my ballets till dawn.

Happy you to be feted in my slim volumes,
monuments I've raised to your beauty.

Extravagant pyramids groping for the stars,
Jove's Olympia temple mimicking Olympus,
the treasures of the original Mausoleum –
none of them is excused a mortal outcome.
Flame or flood will drag down their glories,
or they'll fall under the silent weight of years.
But a name won by inspiration time
cannot destroy: that name is deathless.

III.3

I dreamed I lay
    in Helicon's soft shade,
where the stream struck by Pegasus flows,
and felt the power to mouth the derring-do
of the kings of Alba,
                    a *magnum opus*;
I was dipping my dainty lips
    to the surging waters
where old Ennius once slaked his thirst
before singing of the Curiatii brothers
                and the javelins of the Horatii,
the royal booty brought on Aemilius' barge,
how Fabius' dilly-dallying won the day,
the calamitous battle at Cannae,
            then the gods rewarding worshippers' devotion,
the guardian deities routing Hannibal
    from their Roman home,
Jupiter saved by the honks of geese.

Then Apollo, spotting me from the Castalian copse,
leaned on his golden lyre
            near his grotto and said:

'What's your business with that river? Are you crazy?
    Who told you to get entangled in an epic?
No glory awaits you that way, Propertius:
    small wheels need smooth going, if you want
your book to be kept on a girl's side-table
    to read as she waits alone for her boyfriend.
Why has your pen strayed from its proper margins?
    Don't overload your talent's rowboat.
One oar in the water, the other skimming the beach –
    then you'll be safe; the worst storms are out at sea.'

With that,
        he pointed his ivory plectrum at a place
where a new path was laid along the mossy floor.
A green cave was studded with pebbles,
                drums hung in the hollow rock;
cult objects of the Muses, a terracotta
image of Father Silenus,
                        Pan-pipes;
and Mistress Venus' doves,
                my kind of crowd,
wet their crimson beaks in the Gorgon's pool;
and the nine Wenches of the different arts
turned their gentle hands
            to their special gifts:
one plucked ivy for Bacchic staffs,
        another worked out string accompaniments,
            a third twined roses in both hands.
One of those goddesses touched me
            (from her face, Calliope, I think):

'Be happy to travel in a swan-drawn carriage,
   not ride into combat on a snorting warhorse.
You don't want to be braying alarms on a raucous
   bugle, or letting Mars loose in Hesiod's grove;
or concerned on what battlefield Marius' standard
   is raised, or Rome is smashing Teutonic hordes;
or how the far-flung Rhine, dyed with Swabian blood,
   carries mangled bodies in grieving waters.
No, you'll sing of garlanded lovers at someone's doorstep,
   holding the drunken standards of night-time dalliance,
so anyone needing your skills to cheat scowling husbands
   can charm shut-away girls to come out to play.'

Thus Calliope.
   She reached her hand into the spring
and dabbed my lips
         with water Philitas drank.

III.4

Divine Caesar is pondering hostilities against the wealthy
                     Indians,
his fleet slicing through the narrows of the pearl-bearing sea.
The pay off, Rome, is significant: the ends of the earth are
                  preparing your triumph;
the Tigris and Euphrates will flow according to your dictates;
finally the back of beyond will come under the Western sceptre;
Parthian trophies will get used to Italy's climate.
Forward, ships, billow out you sails of war!
Men, steer your horses toward the customary task.
The omens are favourable. Wipe clean the Crassus debacle.
Godspeed and let Roman history be in your thoughts.

Father Mars, holy Vesta whose fires control the future,
let me survive, I pray, until that dawn
when I see Caesar's chariot loaded with loot,
the spears of the fleeing cavalry, the bows of the Eurasian
                              troops,
the captured leaders sitting beneath their armour,
the horses shying at the clapping of the mob …

And me, I'll be resting on the bosom of my true-love,
watching and reading off the names of the cities we've taken.
Look after your descendant, Venus – may Augustus live
                              forever,
the sole survivor of Aeneas' line.

Let the spoils go to those whose labours have earned them.
I'll be happy just applauding at the roadside.

III.5

Love is the god of peace:
        we lovers worship peace.
I have regular hand-to-hand combat –
        but only with my lover;
I don't grab my food
        from tacky golden plate,
or satisfy my thirst
        from jewel-encrusted cups,
I have no rich country estates,
        ploughed by two thousand oxen,
or any bronzes smelted
        in the sack of Corinth.

What a failure Earth turned out
        for Prometheus its creator,
so careless in his work
        on the human intellect,
so concerned with the body
        he left the brain cavity short,
when the mind's pathways
        should have been set straight first!
Now, heedless of the sea,
        we are tossed by the winds
in search of enemies,
        piling wars on wars.

You won't take any cash
        to the waters of Acheron;
you fool, you will go naked
        on the underworld ferry.
Victor and vanquished rub
        shoulders among the dead:
captured Jugurtha sits
        with consul Marius;
Croesus just at arm's length
        from the beggar Irus.
Carpe diem and then die –
        that is the best way.
I'm glad I worshipped Helicon
        in my early youth
and joined my hands up in
        the dances of the Muses;
I'm glad I occupy
        my mind with lots of wine
and garlands of spring roses
        always adorn my head.

When burdensome time calls
      a halt to my *amours*
and old age sprinkles white
      hairs among the black,
then I'll enjoy learning
      the habits of Mother Nature,
and which god really rules
      this home of ours on earth;
where the rising sun comes from,
      where it goes when it sets,
how it is that the moon
      refills its orb each month;
why gales rule the ocean
      and what the east wind is chasing,
how come there is everlasting
      water to feed the clouds;

whether the day will dawn
      that will uproot fortress Earth,
why the glistening bow
      drinks up the rainwater;
what causes tremors in
      the summits of Mount Pindus
or why the sun mourns and
      eclipse blacks out his horses;
why the starry Ploughman drives
      his oxen and waggon so slowly;
why the Pleiades' chorus
      clusters together in fire;
why the deep ocean
      doesn't spill over its edges
and the year is divided
      into its four seasons;
whether gods hold court in the underworld
      and the wicked are tormented;

whether there are wheels and rocks,
      and thirst amid all that water,
the madness of Alcmaeon
      and the hunger of Phineus;
whether Tisiphone's head
      writhes with black snakes for hair;
whether Cerberus guards
      with three mouths the abyss of hell,
and nine acres are
      too few for Tityus.
Or is it all some fiction
      that oppresses us poor mortals
and there can be no fear
      of anything after the grave?

That is how I shall spend
      my last days; but you who prefer
to make war, off you go and bring
      the standards of Crassus home.

III.6

Oh tell me the truth about my love, Lygdamus,
if you want to escape the chains of a mistress (mine).
For every messenger should be worthy of trust,
especially a vulnerable slave, *a fortiori*.
Anything you recall, I want the whole story
starting at the beginning; I shall be all ears.

So. Did she cry? If so, how many tears
fell from her eyes? Was her hair undone?
Had she not got her mirror out? Was her bed unmade?

No jewel adorning her snow-white fingers?
I warn you, Lygdamus, don't pump me up with false hope,
reporting what you think I want to hear.

'A dowdy dress hung from her delicate shoulders,
and her make-up box was closed at the foot of her bed.
The house was sad, so were her maids, picking up
their spinning tasks, while she wove in the same room,
drying her eyes by pressing the wool against them.
She rejected your accusations indignantly:

"Lygdamus, is this the reward he promised?
(Even slaves can be punished for perjury).
I'm innocent: can he leave me in misery,
with some unspeakable slut kept in his home?
Is he happy I'm wasting away alone in bed?
If he wants to, let him dance, then, on my tomb.

"That hussy wins on herbs, not on performance:
she's got him on her wheel and pulls the strings;
it's the magic powers of toad essence or
bones picked from dried-out snakes that draws him in,
screech-owl feathers found amid fresh graves,
a wool headband snatched from a passing corpse.

"If my dreams come true, Lygdamus, I vow he'll get
his punishment, late but lengthy, at my feet:
a dusty cobweb stretched across his bed:
Venus snoring on their nights together."'

If that's what she honestly said to you, Lygdamus,
run back the same way to her house, fast as you can,
and give her this message, laying on the tears:
I was angry, not deceitful – and I love her;
I too am being roasted on the same fire,

and will swear that I've been celibate twelve days.

Should you manage a happy outcome to our war,
Lygdamus – if it's down to me – you're a free man.

III.7

QED. Money, you *are* the root of all evil.
You take us on a premature last journey,
feeding men's vices with your toxic diet,
seedbed of our neuroses.
You smashed a raging sea time and again
over Paetus sailing to Alexandria.
Chasing you, he's lost in the bloom of youth,
floating, strange fruit for exotic fish.

Let's not stop! Let's lay more hulls, causes
of oblivion, death brought on by human hand!
Land wasn't enough; we added sea, putting
our skills to building more paths to destruction.
Will an anchor hold you if your house could not?
What does he merit who finds his country cramped?
The winds take anything you acquire, no ship
ever made it to old age; harbours deceive.

Tied to boulders in storms overnight,
your ropes frayed, all your moorings failed.
Nature spreads out the sea to trap the grasping:
you might be lucky once, not more.
Kafireas' reefs once broke the victorious fleet
of Greece, driven to wreck in the desolate ocean.
Ulysses mourned his comrades, lost one by one,
his wiles worthless against the waves.

Now Paetus had to hear the storm whistle,
his soft hands rubbed raw by rough cables;
no bedroom of citron-wood or terebinth,
no multi-coloured pillow to prop his head:
that villainous night saw him lie on a tiny plank,
his gasping mouth sucking in the fatal water,
the surge tearing out his still-living nails:
disasters conspired to make Paetus die.

These his final tearful words,
as the black liquor closed over his dying lips:
'Aegean gods, winds that control the seas,
waves pulling down my head, why
are you snatching the doomed years of my youth?
I came to your channels, boyish hair uncut,
to be dashed against sharp rocks where razorbills preen!
Neptune has raised his trident against me.
At least may the swell wash me to Italy,
so my mother may hold whatever is left of me.
But why spell out my age or, as I swim,
speak of my mother? The sea has no gods.'

Then the maelstrom dragged him under –
his last words, his last day.
If he'd been content to turn the soil with the family
oxen, if he'd taken my advice,
he'd be living, happily dining with friends at home,
poor but on *terra firma*, just riches missing.

You sea-nymphs, the hundred daughters of Nereus,
and Thetis, touched by a mother's grief,
you could have cupped his tired chin in your hands:
he'd not have weighed upon your arms.
Sinister North Wind, feared rapist of Orithyia,
what were the great spoils you took from him?

Some trophy – eh, Neptune? – that shattered ship,
the keel that carried those men of religion.

Seagulls hover now above your bones,
the whole Aegean is your cemetery;
your mother can't make offerings at your grave
or inter you in the family vault.
Hand back the body, waves: the sea took his life;
cheap sand, cover Paetus naturally;
and the sailor passing Paetus' sepulchre
will say: 'Even the bold should fear the ocean.'

Cruel North Wind, you'll never see my sails:
mine's a landlubber's tomb at my lady's door.

III.8

What a thrill last night our lamplit battle!
All the abuse of your enraged voice!
Go for it, grab hold of my hair,
dig your designer nails into my face,
threaten to burn my eyes out, tear
my shirt from off my chest! *Un petit verre*
and then you knock the table over, full
glasses come flying at me in your anger:
true love! The signs are unmistakable –
when a female's stressed out, it's the real thing.

Women who throw around foul-mouthed insults
are grovelling at Venus' feet.
One rings herself with bodyguards, one hurtles
like a maenad under the influence down the street,
one's terrorised by mad dreams every night,

one's moved to misery by a girl's portrait –
all proof of passion, Doctor Propertius says
after years of studying love's telltale symptoms.
True commitments are expressed in quarrels.
(I'll leave slow-burning girls to my enemies.)

Competitors can see the bite-marks cover
my neck; bruises are my girlfriend's souvenirs.
Let me feel pain in love, or hear you suffer,
and see my tears or yours.
Give me an angry woman to swoon over.
What fun is sleep when undisturbed by sighs?

Paris sharpened his erotic joy
by pleasuring Helen amid the battle's roar:
the Greeks advanced, Hector fought on for Troy –
Paris' main thrust was 'twixt his lady's thighs…

With you – or about you with rivals – endless war
will be my lot: peace cannot be.
But he who plots to steal you from my bed,
may his house be forever haunted by in-laws!
And any night that he may get gifted
is not for love of him but to spite me.

III.9

Maecenas, sprung from Etruscan kings yet not
ruling-class, always anxious not to tempt fortune,
why launch me on an ocean of versification?
Great billowing sails will not fit my craft.
Putting a weight on one's head that it won't stand,
staggering and giving up – it's humiliating.

Make allowances for muscle power.
Palm trees grow at different elevations.

Lysippus was famed for his 'breathing' human sculptures;
Calamis' boast (for me) is his perfect horses.
Apelles painted the woman he adored as Venus;
Parrhasius plays games in his intricate art.
The pieces from Mentor's smithery tell a story;
those of Mys trail fine acanthus leaves.
Resplendent ivory for Phidias' Jupiter,
while local stone sells Praxiteles.
Some win Olympic medals for chariot-racing;
others gain their kudos in the sprint;
one man's a diplomat, one excels in war:
all cultivate the seeds sown in their souls.

You, Maecenas, could wield the symbols of office,
lay down laws out in the Roman Forum,
or charge through the massed ranks of Parthian bowmen,
then load the walls of your home with captured weapons –
Augustus would give you authority to do it,
easy wealth would flow to you any time ...
Yet you hold back, modestly hug the shadows,
you yourself furl your swelling sails.
Your judgment, trust me, puts you alongside
men like Camillus; people will speak of you,
you'll march to the beat of Caesar's fame,
loyalty the real trophy of Maecenas.

I've taken a leaf from your book, Maecenas,
following your lead so closely I overtake you.
I don't cut the sea-swell in a galleon –
under the banks of a rivulet's where I'm safe.
I'll shed no tears over Thebes' citadel sinking
to warm ashes or the rout of all seven attackers;

I'll not report on the gates and towers of Troy,
the ten summers before the Greeks sailed home
after the city walls had been ploughed over
by the wooden horse fashioned by Minerva.
I'll just give pleasure from Callimachus' library,
write in Philitas' metre – that's enough.
Let these writings set the young ablaze –
they can call me a god, bring me offerings!

You should flex the reins to steer my youth,
give direction to my rolling wheels;
if you showed the way, I'd write of Jupiter's wars,
the giants threatening heaven from Thessaly;
I'd relate how Rome's bulls grazed the Palatine,
how Remus' murder strengthened the ramparts,
the twin kings suckled at a wild beast's teat,
my genius growing to match your commands;
I'd hail the triumphal chariots from east and west,
the arrows fired in the Parthians' crafty flight,
Egyptian bastions toppled by Roman steel,
Antony's death by his own hand…

As it is, Maecenas, you bring me praise: it's thanks
to you that people say I have joined your ranks.

III.10

I wondered why the Muses smiled
standing beside my bed at the blush of sunrise:
to celebrate the birthday of my girl,
clapping three times to bring her luck.
I want a cloudless day, the winds at standstill,
waves pattering safely on the shore.

No one's to grieve today,
Niobe's rock will dry her tears,
halcyons cease lugubrious cries,
the nightingale refrain from mourning.

You, darling, favoured by your birth-signs,
rise, pray to gods for just rewards,
wash off sleep with pure spring water,
style your bright hair between your fingers.
Slip on that dress that first caught my eye,
keep a garland round your head.
Ask that your beauty lasts forever
and your power to rule me never fails.

When incense drifts from flower-decked altars,
and propitious flames burn through the house,
think of nightfall, the time for feasting, drinking,
saffron pot-pourris that tease your nostrils.
The flute-playing fades into dancing,
risqué talk stirs your appetites,
amorous tiffs hold sleep at bay,
the street outside echoes to the noise.

We'll throw dice to decide which of us
is smacked the harder by Cupid's wing.
Then when enough cups have been downed,
Venus conducts the night-time rituals
we'll observe in our bedroom:
your birthday's climax.

III.11

No surprises if a woman drives my life
or holds me, a man, subject to her laws;
you accuse me of being a worthless failure
because I can't break the chains, shatter the yoke.
I used to talk like that in my younger days:
now I say – learn from my example.

Medea clamped a yoke of carbon steel
on fire-breathing bulls, sowed armed men in the ground,
shut the mouth of the guardian snake
so the golden fleece could go home with Jason.

Penthesilea, the Russian, fired arrows from
horseback against the Greek armada;
when her gold helmet was stripped from her face,
her beauty slew her slayer.

Omphale, bathed in the gold-bearing Lydian lake,
rose so high in beauty's hall of fame
she had him who brought world peace and raised the Pillars
put his horny hand to the spinning wheel.

Semiramis built the city of Babylon,
a solid piece of work with baked brick walls
so wide two chariots could pass on top
without touching axle hubs.
She channelled the Euphrates through her citadel
and made Central Asia bend to her rule.

Why put heroes in the dock or even gods?
(Jupiter brings disrepute on himself and his house).
What of him who blotted our army's honour?
Or **That Woman** serviced by her manservants?

The price she set for her obscene marriage was
Rome's walls and our senators plighted to her kingdom.
Noxious Alexandria's a fertile seedbed
for treachery; Egyptian sand that soaked up
so much of our blood robbed Pompey of three triumphs.
There's no day can wipe out Rome's infamy;
better he had died at Pharsalus than there,
even with neck bowed to his father-in-law.

The bitch-queen from the fleshpots of the Delta
(what else do you expect from the Macedon line?)
tried to set baying Anubis on Jupiter,
menace the Tiber with the Nile,
drive back the Roman trumpet with the tambourine,
chase our warships with felucca poles,
hang smelly mosquito nets on the Tarpeian rock,
legislate among Marius' trophies on the Capitol.
Pointless to have smashed the power of Tarquin,
proud by nature, Proud by name,
if **She** was to be endured. Saved Rome should chant
Augustus' triumph, pray his life be long.
She fled to the Nile's meandering mouths,
held out her hands for Roman shackles,
watched the sacred asps bite her arms,
and her limbs start on sleep's long road to nowhere.
'With such a leader, how could you fear me?'
she said, her tongue thick with wine...

The city high on seven hills oversees the world...
The gods founded its walls and still protect them:
with Caesar here, why would Rome fear Jove?
Don't talk of Scipio's fleets, Camillus' standards
or those Pompey captured at the Bosphorus,
the spoils seized from Hannibal and beaten Syphax,
or Pyrrhus' glory shivered at our feet.

Curtius won his statue plugging a gap;
Decius broke enemy ranks spurring his horse;
Horatius' alley recalls the hacked-down bridge;
a crow gave Corvinus a permanent name.
Apollo on Levkas will tell how the battle lines
were turned: one day's war ended so much.

Sailor, whether steering for port or leaving it,
think Caesar right across the Ionian Sea.

III.12

How could you, Postumus? Leave a pleading Galla
to go off soldiering under Augustus' standards?
Was the glory of Parthian spoils of so much value
her entreaties merited such disregard?
You gold-diggers all, may I say, deserve one fate,
or anyone preferring war to true love's bed.
You're mad to wearily drink from your helmet
Aras water, a filthy cloak over your head,
while Galla's nerves are frayed by stupid rumours
that you've served with utmost bravery – but you're dead,
slain by a chain-mailed knight upon an armoured
horse, or a Persian arrow spilled your blood,
and what's left to cry over's coming in a pot
(a common means of transport from those parts).
You're truly blessed in the woman you've got –
three or four times more than your just deserts.
What does a girl do when her husband's left,
seeing Rome instructs her in debauchery's art?
Don't worry: Galla won't be won by gifts
and won't remember your hardness of heart.
Whenever fate returns you in one piece,

loyal Galla will wrap your neck round in her arms.
For your admirable spouse they'll compare you to Ulysses –
lengthy delays never did *him* any harm:
ten years' war, the Cicones killed when Ismara fell,
the Cyclops' eye burnt to eternal night,
Circe's tricks, the lotus' magic spells,
Scylla and Charybdis raging in and out,
Lampetie's cattle still heard, on spits, to low
(she'd pastured them for her father, the Sun),
flight from the chamber of weeping Calypso,
winter nights and days just swimming on,
visiting the silent souls' twilight home,
passing the Sirens' lyres with crew deafened,
the old bow dusted off for suitor doom,
and so his wandering came to an end:
all worth it for that wifely chastity.

And constant Galla outstrips Penelope.

III.13

Why do grasping women make nights so pricey
(you ask), why are fortunes lost through venery?
There's one manifest cause for all these crashes:
the road to luxury has been made too easy.
Indian miner-ants excavate gold,
pearls are born from ocean foam like Venus,
Tyre exports its purple dyes,
Arab spice-growers bring cinnamon:
such weaponry storms any girl's castle walls,
overwhelms a Penelope's disdain.
Housewives parade dressed in the wealth of toyboys,
the in-your-face spoils of their degradation.

The courteous rituals of asking, giving,
are gone: the wallet ends all hesitation.

The Indian, bronzed in dawn's waters,
enjoys a felicitous funeral law.
When the torch is thrown into his pyre,
there stands a pious crowd of wives, hair loose,
contesting who, still living, will follow
her husband: not to die is a disgrace.
The winner exults, clasping the flames to her breast,
pressing her burnt lips to her man's.
No brides like that round here, no woman
a loyal Evadne or Penelope.

The young lived quietly once in the country,
their bank accounts the harvest and the tree.
Presents were quinces shaken from the branch,
panniers filled with purple blackberries,
hand-picked violets, a mix of lilies
shining in their wicker baskets,
grapes brought on the vine,
a bird of multi-coloured plumage.
For these emoluments the girls rewarded
rural men in discreet hollows,
a fawn-skin blanket for the clinching lovers
on natural, thick grass beds,
a stooping pine shading them where they lay.
The ram spontaneously led well-fed ewes
back to the Arcadian shepherd's unlocked pen.

Seeing goddesses naked was no crime;
divinities of both genders guarding the fields
spoke kindly, altars were benign:
'Out for hares, my friend, whoever you are,
or birds, perhaps, in my valley?

Call me, Pan, from the cliff to go with you,
whether you hunt prey with limed twigs or dogs.'

The groves are deserted now, the shrines closed,
religion dead, gold the new deity.
Gold has driven out trust, gold buys justice,
law chases gold: no law means no conscience.
The charred door testified to Brennus' sacrilege
when he attacked Apollo's sanctuary:
Parnassus, shaken to its bay-crowned summit,
spewed an avalanche on the Gallic army.
Thracian Polymestor was a godless
host, pocketing Polydorus' gold.
And Amphiaraus vanished with his horses
for the golden bangles on Eriphyla's arms.
I'll say it – and I hope I'm a false prophet:
its wealth will be proud Rome's decline and fall.
I'm right, but no one listens.
                              Well, Cassandra
should have been believed about the fall of Troy;
she alone said Paris would seal its fate
and the horse slithering inside was a trick.
Her 'ravings' could have saved her land, her father;
her unheeded tongue proved the gods don't lie.

III.14

Your gyms, Sparta, have many admirable features,
but especially the exercising of young wenches;
for you see no harm in sports where a girl strips off
and trains her body alongside male athletes.

The ball flies from hand to hand,
the hooked stick clatters on the rolling hoop;
a woman stands at the finish-line covered in dust,
or gets a bruise or two in the all-in wrestling;
she happily straps the boxing-gloves on her forearms,
swings the heavy discus to hurl; pounds
the ring on horseback, a sword at her white flank,
a bronze helmet shielding her maidenly head,
like a warring squadron of topless Amazons
roaming the Turkish plains.

Sometimes she follows the Spartan hounds down the ridges
of Taygetus, her hair sprinkled with frost.
Or think Castor and Pollux on the banks of Eurotas,
one a winner with horses, the other with fists,
and Helen taking up arms with them, breasts bare,
not blushing – they say – before her immortal brothers.

Spartan law calls for no segregation of lovers,
you can be beside your woman in the street;
no need to fear a guard on a locked-up girl
or the crushing retaliation of a jealous man:
no need for a go-between, you can speak yourself
of your business, and no rebuffs after lengthy delays.
No foreign fashions to trick the roving eye
or tiresome styling of hair drenched in scent.

But Roman girls go out hemmed in by a mob,
the street so packed you can't get a fingertip through;
which ones are approachable, which fob you off with words,
you'll never find out: the lover treads a blind alley.
If you followed Spartan laws (not to say their sports),
I'd be much fonder of you, Rome, for that.

III.15

When I put away boyhood clothing, and inhibitions
too, I was free to explore the paths of love;
Lycinna, who asked for nothing in return,
partnered my first nights, refining my unschooled urges.
In the few years that have passed since then, as I
recall, I've barely exchanged ten words with her.
Your love buried everything, no woman after
draped her sweet chains about my neck ...
Don't let any gossip about me trouble your ears,
I shall love only you even on the funeral pyre,
as I hope the course of that love will run smooth
and no night will come when I lie awake without you.
Hell hath no fury, etcetera, I know,
but leave Lycinna alone – she doesn't deserve it.

Exemplum: Dirce was enraged by claims
(true enough) that Antiope had bedded Lycus.
Many a time the queen tore out Antiope's
beautiful hair and slapped her soft face hard.
She loaded her maid with impossible tasks,
made her lay her head on the rough ground,
gave her dark, dank quarters to live in,
even denied her a miserable cup of water.
Jupiter, why could you not help Antiope in
her time of need, the hard chain bruising her hands?
Call yourself a god, you should be ashamed your girl
was a slave in bondage: who else could she turn to?

Alone, she summoned all her body's strength
and broke the queen's shackles from both her wrists.
Fearfully she scaled the peaks of Mount Cithaeron;
it was night, frost sprinkled her wretched bed.
A river's indistinct rush terrified her,

sounding like her mistress after her.
She was driven from the mountain shelter – a mother's
tears left Zethus unmoved, though Amphion softened.
As, when the churning sea is stilled
and the south and north winds cease going head to head,
the sound of sand sucked down the shore subsides,
Antiope bowed her knees and fell.

Pity at last; her sons saw their mistake.
The old man, fit to rear Jove's offspring,
gave the boys back their mother; and those boys
tied Dirce to a wild bull's head for dragging.
Jupiter's doing, Antiope: you won;
Dirce was pulled to die in many places.
Blood soaked Zethus' fields; Amphion sang
a victory ode from the crag of Aracynthus.

III.16

Her letter reaches me at midnight,
summoning me *now* (if not sooner) to Tivoli,
where white-roofed towers bestride
the Aniene's plunge to spreading pools.

What to do? Sally forth in pitch darkness
and risk violent hands around my throat?
Yet if that fear makes me delay her order,
her tears will hurt me more than nocturnal hoodlums.
I made that mistake once. Result: a year's rejection.
It'll be *her* hands that won't be gentle with me.

Wait, though. Lovers are sacred – no one will harm them:
they can walk down the middle of Sciron's street.

You're in love? You can stroll in the badlands of Scythia:
who would be such a barbarian as to strike you?
Anaemic lovers' blood wouldn't even stain
a villain; Venus rides bodyguard for her own.
The moon lights the way, the stars pick out the hazards,
Amor goes ahead, waving blazing torches;
mad dogs keep their jaws to themselves.
The road is always safe for such a traveller.

Even if my adventure led to certain death,
such an end would be worth a high price to me.
She would bring perfume, decorate my tomb
with garlands, keep watch sitting at my gravestone.
I pray she does not bury me in a crowded spot
where the mob tramps by on some thoroughfare.
That would desecrate a lover's resting place.
Let tree leaves shade me in secluded ground,
or inter me amid anonymous sand dunes.
I don't want my name displayed at the roadside.

III.17

I kneel, Bacchus, at your altar,
fill my sails with breezes, father,
    you who know the shoals of love;
witness Ariadne, carried,
Bacchus, by your lynx-drawn chariot
    to sidereal life above.

You can quell the storms of Venus,
heal our wounds with medicine vinous,
    join or sever loving pairs:
wash this cancer from my spirit

(either death or wine must cure it),
   cleanse my bones of those old fires.

Sober nights rack lonely lovers,
hope and fear supplant each other.
   But if your gift conjures sleep,
warming my brain with its ardour,
I'll sow hills with vines in order,
   which no birds or beasts can strip.

Cellar vats will foam with purple,
new grapes stain the feet that trample –
   my remaining life is yours.
I'll be singer of your virtues,
tell of lightning bolts that birthed you,
   Indian troops routed by choirs,

vines that roused Lycurgus' tantrums,
Pentheus slain by massed Bacchantes,
   and the tendrilled vessel's crew,
turned to arching dolphins, diving,
crowds of Naxos folk imbibing
   fragrant streams of your rich brew.

I'll drape you with ivy wreathing,
crown you with a tarboosh, smoothing
   scented oil round your soft throat;
barefoot, your long robe vibrating,
you'll hear Theban drums pulsating,
   goat-foot Pan playing on the flute.

Great Cybele with her raucous
cymbals leads the dancing chorus,
   she who gave our cities towers;

priests marking your solemn rituals
pour libations from gold pitchers,
   standing at your temple doors –

rites that I shall be narrating
driven by the same afflatus
   that inspired Pindar in Greece,
if you'll only liberate me
from her who humiliates me:
   grant me pure unconsciousness!

III.18

The playful sea, end-stopped by tree-fringed Averno,
steaming pools, warm water overflowing,
where Aeneas' trumpeter lies in Cuma sands
and the waves sound across Hercules' road –
here cymbals once clashed for Bacchus of Thebes
making his benevolent way to Italian cities.

But now, what malign god halted at your waters,
Baia, your name a curse on everyone's lips?
Marcellus plunged his face into Styx' ripples,
a ghost wandering by the underworld lake.
Pedigree, courage, matchless mother,
the embrace of Caesar's home – all valueless.
Awnings fluttering above the capacity crowd
at the stadium, everything those young hands achieved?
He died. Time stood still in his twentieth year,
sealing so much good in so small a compass.

Go, give your spirits a lift, imagine triumphs,
a standing ovation from the whole theatre;

wear cloth of gold or finer, everything studded
with Indian pearls: you'll give the lot to the flames.
Forget class or caste, there's just one destination:
the road's bad, but everyone must tramp it;
those three baying dog's mouths must be appeased,
the grim greybeard's ferry boarded (no private yacht).
Let a man barricade himself with steel or bronze,
death will still drag him from his hiding place.
Strength did not exempt Achilles or beauty Nireus,
nor the wealth washed down by the Pactolus rescue Croesus.

May the sailor who conveys the souls
of the righteous carry your lifeless body
where Claudius, victor of Sicily, and Julius
forked off the human road to climb *ad astra*.

III.19

You cast our male libido in my face.
Trust me, you women are more that way inclined.
Once break the bonds of shame, you cannot
restrain the female mind.

Fire will sooner damp down in a cornfield,
rivers run backwards to their fountainheads,
Sirt offer safe harbour, treacherous Malea
extend a friendly greeting to passing sailors,
than your depravity could be reined in,
your sexual passion's goading blunted.

Take her whose love the Cretan bull rejected
so donned the fake horns of a fir-wood cow;
or Tyro, burning for a river,

who gave her all to Neptune turned to water.

What of Medea, whose mother-love
appeased her anger with her children's slaughter,
or that adultery which plunged
Mycenae's palace into infamy?
Then Myrrha's craving for her aged father –
until she sprouted leaves. Another crime.

And Scylla sold her father's kingdom,
shearing his magic hair for Minos' beauty:
a dowry she'd promised the enemy.
Love opened Nisus' gates, but in deceit.
Brides, may your wedding torches burn more brightly
than hers: a Cretan ship dragged her down.
Minos rightly is now a judge in hell:
he won, but acted by his enemy well.

III.20

Think he can still remember how you look,
the one you saw sail off from your embrace?
A hard man to swap his girl for lucre.
Was all Africa worth one teardrop down your face?
Pure folly to trust the gods or his empty words:
he's probably clasping a new love to his chest.

You have potent beauty and the skills of chaste
Minerva, the glitter of a learned ancestor.
All your house needs to be blest is a true partner;
I will be him: darling, come lie with me.
Sun, who spin out your fire longer in summer,
shorten the journey of your lingering light;

my first night is coming, give time for a first night.
Moon, wait on our first union before you set.
How many hours will we talk away
till Venus spurs us to our sweet combat!

Terms must be settled, pens put to a deal,
my new *amour* needs statutes written down.
Love will enshrine the pledges with his seal,
witnessed by Ariadne's starry crown.
A union that no compact binds
brings no gods to avenge the insomnia;
where lust ties bonds, those bonds will soon unwind:
may our love be sustained by its first aura.

Let him who breaks vows sworn upon the altar
and stains the marriage sacrament in another's
arms suffer the pains common to lovers;
let sharp-tongued gossip swirl about his head,
his mistress close her windows to his tears:
eternal love eternally frustrated.

III.21

I must take the grand tour to Athens, seat of learning,
hoping love's burden shakes free on the long road.
Infatuation grows from constant looking
at the girl; Amor feeds upon himself.
I've tried every trick to escape – nothing helps:
still I'm harassed by the insomniac god.
After frequent refusals, she lets me in once or twice,
or visits and sleeps fully clothed on the edge of the bed.
There's just one hope: a change of country – Cynthia
out of sight, out of mind.

Step to it, boys, push the boat out to deep water,
form into pairs and take shifts at the oars;
hoist the mainsail up the mast for clear skies:
the breeze promises sailors a smooth voyage.
Goodbye to my friends and to the towers of Rome,
and you, whatever you mean to me, girl, goodbye.

I'm a first-time guest of Adriatic foam,
it's the turn of marine deities to hear my prayer.
Then, across the Ionian Sea, when my yacht has rested
its tired sails in the calm of Corinth port,
feet, take the strain for what's next, where the dry
land of the isthmus holds two seas apart.
When Piraeus harbour has welcomed me ashore,
I'll climb the long ridge of the Athens road.

There I'll improve my mind in the colonnade
of Plato or gardens of the sage Epicurus;
or study Demosthenes' weapon, the edge of the tongue,
and taste the salt of elegant Menander;
certainly feast my eyes on a famous painting
or two, the odd ivory or bronze sculpture.
The passing of years, the sea's separation of us
will quietly heal the fissures in my heart;
if I die, it'll be by fate, not a worthless love affair;
the day of such a death will come with honour.

III.22

How many years is it you've enjoyed cool Cyzicus,
Tullus, the isthmus in the Sea of Marmara,
Cybele carved from sacred vine-wood,
the road Pluto drove for his wife-snatching?

I don't begrudge you the cities of the Dardanelles,
certainly the swans on the Cayster are to be seen,
and the serpentine channels of meandering Maeander ...
but just spare a thought for how much I miss you,
Tullus.

Perhaps you'll see Atlas propping up the sky,
Medusa's head chopped off by Perseus,
the ox-stalls of Geryon, the marks in the dust
from Hercules' and Antaeus' wrestling match,
the places where Hesperus' daughters danced;
or maybe you'll sail to the river of Colchis,
retracing the whole voyage of the Argo,
raw pine turned into something new – a ship,
which slid between the rocks behind a dove.

Roman soil can outdo all these wonders:
Anything that's anywhere – you'll find it here,
a land of martial strength yet not of villainy:
the historical record won't be ashamed of Rome.
Our power is less in cold steel than
in decency, a controlled anger in victory.

For water, we have Tivoli's Aniene,
Clitunno from the Umbrian uplands,
Marcius' everlasting aqueduct,
Lake Albano, Nemi among the leaves,
and the wholesome spring drunk by Pollux' horse.

No cobras here, slithering on scaly bellies;
Italian seas don't seethe with monsters;
no Andromeda rattling her chains in place of her mother;
no banquets in Italy that repel the sun;
no death sentences by long-distance fire,
imposed by mothers on their sons;

no vicious Bacchae hunt Pentheus in a tree,
no substituted deer launch a Greek fleet;
here Juno never put horns on her rival
or spoiled her beauty with a horrid cow's face.
This, Tullus, is your mother, the *bel paese*,
here office befitting your venerable family,
citizens to hear your oratory, the prospect of
much progeny, the proper love of a wife-to-be.

III.23

My writing tablets disappeared somewhere,
and many a masterpiece gone with them!
Worn by my daily fingerprints,
even without my seal unmistakably mine.
They could placate girls when I failed to show,
fobbing them off with some persuasive line.
No gold embossing to make them valuable,
just cheap wax in a frame of common pine.
Still, they always were my loyal servants,
always producing excellent results.

A typical note they brought me might have been:
'I'm furious with you for being late yesterday.
You found some other, prettier lady, right?
You made up something bad I'm supposed to have done?'
Or else: 'Please come today, we'll have some fun:
there'll be a loving welcome through the night' –
the clever things a willing girl will say
to pass an hour with gentle repartee.

Oh no! Some miser's stowing them away
among his ledgers, filled with his accounts!

I'll pay in gold if someone hands them in.
Cash for just bits of wood? Who could decline?
Go, boy, and stick this notice on some column.
My address? Just say: 'The Esquiline'.

III.24–25

Your trust in your beauty, woman, is misplaced:
it was my poems once made you arrogant.
My love, Cynthia, heaped such praises on you,
my verse left you embarrassingly well known.
I gathered many women's charms in you,
when infatuation made you what you weren't;
I compared you often to the roseate dawn,
though you'd contrived the freshness of your face.

I was forced to say it by love's branding-iron.
I was shipwrecked in Aegean waters, taken
captive, hands twisted behind my back,
roasted alive in Venus' cauldron.
Friends and family could not save me, nor
the witches of Thessaly cleanse with an ocean.
                                                    But look!
My garlanded ship has now touched harbour,
the shoals are passed and I have dropped anchor.

I'm convalescing, tired of the sea's huge swell;
finally my wounds have closed and healed.
I pledge myself to the goddess of Good Sense,
if there is one: Jove was deaf to my appeals.
They laughed at me where tables were laid out;
anyone could gossip at my expense.
Five years I served you loyally: you will bite

your lip remembering my constancy.

Tears will not help: you used them to ensnare me;
it's always a trick, Cynthia, when you cry.
I'll cry too as I leave, but the harm lasts longer:
ours was a team – you wouldn't make it work.
Your very threshold wept for me – goodbye
to the door my angry fist could never break.

May age weigh on you as imperceptible years
slide past, and lines disfigure your skin;
your turn then to endure sneers of rejection,
shut out, a crone sorry she was once so haughty.
My page has sung its fateful curse upon you.
Fear the end that is to come – even to your beauty.

BOOK FOUR

IV.1

Everything you see here, friend, where the megacity of Rome
now stands was hills and grass till Trojan Aeneas settled,
and where the Palatine rises, sacred to Apollo,
was a mating-ground for exiled Evander's cattle.
These gilded temples grew from pottery deities,
no one was ashamed to live in an artless shack,
Jupiter thundered from the bare Tarpeian Rock
and immigrant Tiber marked our boundary-walls.
Now Romulus' home is mounted up on steps;
once, just a hearth was all the brothers' kingdom.
Parliament, this gleaming mansion for togaed deputies,
used to house elders in skins, rustic souls;
a shepherd's horn called the ancient Romans into session:
the Senate was a hundred men in a fenced meadow;
no cavernous theatres were hung with swirling drapes,
no stages reeked of ceremonial saffron.

Nobody was concerned to run after foreign gods,
just pendulant figurines in a local rite;
Vesta was poor, and proud of her garlanded donkeys;
scrawny cows led cheap ceremonies;
pigs were fattened to sacrifice at a few crossroads,
and a herdsman offered sheep's entrails, playing the pipe.
The leather-clad ploughman plied his bristly whip,
precursor of dubious Lupercalia rituals;
raw recruits did not glitter in menacing armour-plate –
they used burnt staves to fight naked battles.

Lycmon in his cap pitched the first staff headquarters;
much of Tatius' military action was over sheep.
This was the age of the old tribes – Tities, Ramnes,
Luceres; of Romulus driving four white horses.
Bovillae was less suburban with a small city,

Gabii a metropolis (it's nothing now),
Alba a power, foretold by the white sow,
and going to Fidene was a major trip.
A son of Rome inherits the name alone,
not thinking a wolf suckled his forefathers.
That wolf was the perfect nurse for our polity:
her milk was fertile – look what bulwarks have grown!

Here Troy sent its guardian spirits for better futures,
good auguries sped the boatload of refugees.
The omens boded well, for the open stomach
of the fir horse left those gods unscathed
when a trembling father clung to his son's neck
and the flames feared to burn the filial shoulders.
That boat brought Decius' heroism, Brutus' axes,
Venus came with her progeny Caesar's weaponry,
the victorious weaponry of Troy rebirthed;
fortunate the land that harboured Julus' deities.
Sitting by Averno, the quivering Sibyl
said Remus' blood must purify the soil;
Cassandra's forecasts were brought to the ears
of aged Priam and proved true in time;
I'll prophesy too: 'Troy falls, Trojan Rome
rises.' I'll tell of sunlit realms of land and sea.
'Roll back the horse, you Greeks. Your victory's
worthless. Ilium will live. Jupiter will arm these cinders.'

Ennius can twine a rough garland for his words:
Bacchus, give me a spray of your ivy plant.
I'm trying to build ramparts in dutiful verse:
damn it, the sound is so small in my mouth!
However miserable, though, the trickle from
my little lungs, it all will serve my home –
Umbria can swell with pride in my writing,
Umbria, home of the Latin Callimachus.

Let people seeing those towers climbing out
of the valleys judge the walls by my genius.
Rome, help me: this poem's for you; citizens, grant
good omens, may bird calls be auspicious as I begin:
rites, gods, old place-names – of these I shall sing:
my horse must sweat its way towards that line.

* * * * * * * *

'Whoa! Not so fast! You're rash to look in the future,
Propertius! The Fates are frowning on your plan.
It will end in tears: Apollo is singing a different tune;
you're plucking words you'll regret from an unwilling lyre.

'My predictions are certain, my sources impeccable – or
I'm a seer who can't even handle an astrolabe.
From the line of Archytas, Orops of Babylon sired me:
Horos, whose house boasts Conon as ancestor.
The gods will witness I've upheld family
traditions – truth comes first in my almanacs.
These days the gods are a cash cow, their king
misinterpreted for gold, like the signs of the zodiac,
the planets – benign Jupiter, ravening Mars,
or Saturn, baleful to everything,
what Pisces portends, or rampant Leo's stars,
or Capricorn, washed by Atlantic waves.

'When Arria packed her twin sons off to battle,
giving them weapons despite divine veto,
it was I who said they would not bring their spears back:
two graves now confirm my truthfulness.
Lupercus, protecting his horse, hit in the muzzle,
saved his fallen mount's life, not his own.
Gallus, guarding the standards of the legion,
died in front of his eagle's blood-stained beak.

Two star-crossed boys, victims of mother's avarice:
I wish I could not say: I told you so.

'And when Cinara's labour pains were dragging on
and the bundle in her womb was holding back,
it was I who said: "Make Juno a vow she can't refuse."
She gave birth: another triumph for my books.
You won't get this service from Jupiter's sandy cave
in Libya, entrails speaking the secrets of heaven,
observations of the wingbeats of a raven,
or some spirit rising from a magic basin.
You must watch the path of the sky, the road of truth
through the stars, put trust in the five zones.

'Calchas is instructive: he untied the fleet
that wisely clung to Aulis' rocky shores;
he stained a blade on the neck of Agamemnon's
daughter, and the king spread blood-red sails.
But the Greeks did not return: demolished Troy
with one glance at the Gulf of Evia staunched its tears.
Nauplius lit fires of vengeance in the night
and Greece sank under the weight of its own spoils.
Triumphant Ajax, take the prophetess and enjoy,
tearing her from Minerva's sheltering gown.

'So much for history; now your horoscope:
brace yourself to face fresh challenges.
Old Umbria produced you from distinguished stock
(am I wrong or is that your native landscape?)
where mist coats dew on the Bevagna plain
and the Umbrian lake's waters warm up in summer;
you gathered bones you were too young to gather –
your father's – and had to live with modest means;
many oxen had worked your fields but the pitiless
bailiff's rod gave away your rich cropland.

When you took childhood's gold amulet off your neck
and donned a man's toga in your mother's home,
Apollo taught you snatches of his music, banned
you ranting in the lunatic Forum.

'"Write love poems: treacherous work, but it's your mission,
and the rest of the crowd will scribe by your example.
You're in Venus' army, wielding her soft-edged weapons,
a worthy sparring-partner for her boys.
And whatever trophies you may land,
one girl will always slip through your palms;
she'll shake your hook out of her mouth as though
it had never been, and her jaws will come after *you*.
Your night, your day will be whatever she says;
no tear fall from your eyes but by her command.
Put a thousand guards on her house, seal up her door –
no use: all a woman needs to cheat is one crack."

'Whether your boat tosses in the ocean,
or you stray, defenceless, among armed men,
or the earth opens wide in some temblor,
beware the eight-footed Crab's sinister back!'

IV.2

One body, so many shapes.
The age-old features of the god Vertumnus.
I'm Tuscan, from Tuscany, but I'm not sorry
I left Etruria when war raged.
I like the crowd here;
I don't want an ivory temple:
a view of the Roman Forum will do for me.
Old Tiber once flowed this way – legend has it

you could hear the oar-plash through the shallows;
once he made a land-grant to the community,
they said I was called VERTumnus
after the stream's diVERTing;
or, because we pluck fruit in auTUMN,
it was thought to be VerTUMNus' rite.
Idle chit-chat, wrong about my name;
the god himself is the only reliable source.

I have the gift of assuming any figure:
whatever you turn me into,
I'll look good.
Dress me in silk – I'll be a compliant girl.
A toga? No one's disputing my virility.
Give me a scythe, a bent straw in my mouth,
you'd say I'd just been mowing the fields.
I put on armour once – they complimented
my performance, I remember.
But I was a harvester too, weighed down with a pannier.
In court, I'm sober as the judge,
but put a garland on me,
you'll shout out that the wine's gone to my head.
In a turban, I can be confused with Bacchus;
or Apollo, with a plectrum in my hand.
With nets I'm a hunter; with a limed twig
the bird-catcher am I.
Vertumnus can also be a charioteer,
a trick rider leaping from horse to horse.
In an angling hat I cast for fish,
in a baggy suit I'm a travelling salesman.
I can lean on my crook as a shepherd, hawk roses
from a wicker basket by the dusty roadside.

Do I need to underline
my principal claim to fame –

the gifts of the garden from my green fingers?
The cucumber bears my stamp, the pot-bellied marrow,
the cabbage tied with rush twine;
I make early grapes redden in clusters,
the spiky corn-ear swell with milky grain;
see these sweet cherries, those late-season plums,
the gleam of blackberries on a summer day;
this necklace of fruit is a grafting job done,
when a reluctant pear tree puts forth apples;
no flower opens in the fields that did not
first decorously droop across my forehead.

Yet I, master of every form,
when the Etruscan force arrived to help,
crushing fierce Tatius' Sabine army,
saw front lines buckling, weapons dropped,
the enemy turn in ignominious flight;
my homeland's language named me from that action,
Rome paid back my Tuscans,
so the Vicus Tuscus has its name today.
Father of the gods, let the Roman crowd,
in their togas, pass my feet for evermore.

Six lines left; I'll not detain you as you hurry
to your court hearing: this is the home straight.

I WAS A MAPLE TRUNK, RUDELY CARVED WITH A SICKLE,
A POOR GOD IN A POOR TOWN BEFORE NUMA'S DAY.
MAMURRIUS, WHO MOULDED ME IN BRONZE,
MAY CAMPANIA'S EARTH SPARE YOUR SKILLED HANDS,
WHICH MADE ME PLIABLE FOR SO MANY USES.
ONE WORK, RECEIVING MULTIPLE HONOURS.

IV.3

Arethusa to her husband Lycotas
(if 'her' is the right term, seeing you're away so often).

Should you notice a gap in the writing as you read,
assume that part has been blotted out by tears;
should you fail to make out some garbled words,
that will show my right hand was faltering.

One day Afghan archers have you in their sights,
the next it's a steel-plated soldier on a warhorse,
freezing Bulgaria, the painted chariots of Britain,
some swarthy Indian scalded by Orient seas . . .

Is this spousal devotion? Was this in our marital vows
when I gave you my unskilled body for your urgent needs?
The torch in my wedding procession to your home
sucked black light from an overturned funeral pyre,
I was sprinkled with Styx-water, my hair-band was crooked,
the marriage god boycotted the proceedings.

All gates sport my offerings – and much good they did me!
I'm now on the fourth cloak woven for your campaigns.
Death to him who cuts helpless trees to build fortifications
or shapes hollow bones into mournful martial trumpets!
He deserves more than Ocnus does to sit twining rope,
forever feeding the hunger of the donkey.

Doesn't that breast-plate blister your sensitive shoulders?
That heavy spear chafe your unwarlike hands?
Better those pains than that some girl's teeth
leave love-bites on your neck that will make me cry.
Poor food, they say, has made you thin in the face:
I'd rather your pallor came from missing me.

As for me, when evening gives way to depressing night,
I kiss any armour of yours that's left lying around.
I complain that the blanket slides off
(though I've got the whole bed)
and the birds haven't got around to their dawn chorus.

On winter nights I work on your camp gear,
weaving Tyrian wool I've chosen for your cloaks;
read up on the Aras River you're supposed to capture,
how far Parthian camels can run without water,
which countries are frozen solid, which crack in the heat,
which wind brings ships safely to Italy.

What use to me is fancy imported clothing,
or translucent jewelry to adorn my hands?
The doorway is quiet, maybe once a month
a girlfriend opens it to visit me,
and it's nice to hear the whimper of my puppy
(she's claimed your side of the bed now for her own).
Just my sister sits with me, and the nurse, pale with worry
at your delay: 'Must be the bad weather,' she lies.

Hippolyte had it easy: bared her chest,
took up arms, put a helmet round her gentle head.
But then she was a foreigner…
If only Roman camps were open to women!
I'd have gone as your trusty kitbag on your campaign.
I'd skip over the mountains of Scythia, when Jupiter
sends frost to turn the deepest waters to pack-ice.

Love is always great, but when they draft your spouse
it's greater; Venus herself keeps the torch burning.
I cover shrines with flowers, smother crossroads with foliage,
Sabine herbs crackle in the old fireplace.
If an owl hoots, perched on a nearby rooftop,

or the slow-burning lamp needs a touch of wine,
that day will spell doom for this year's lambs
and the priest's men will tie on their robes in their zeal for
                                        fresh cash.

Don't let storming Afghan ramparts be so important,
or stripping some perfumed general of his linen robes,
when the whirling sling launches its lead weights
and the crafty bow twangs from retreating horsemen;
I hope you do subdue the Parthian troops
and carry the conqueror's spear on your triumphal chariot –
just so long as you keep our marriage vows unblemished:
on that one condition I pray you make it home;
when I hang up your weapons at the Capena Gate,
I'll sign: A GIRL SAVED BY HER MAN'S SAFE RETURN.

IV.4

The Tarpeian grove, the shaming tomb of Tarpeia will be
    my theme, and the capture of Jupiter's ancient threshold.
Imagine Rome at that time, when a trumpeter from Cures
    rattled Jove's crags with a lengthy blast.
Where laws are now dictated for subjugated lands
    in the Roman Forum, Sabine spears stood.
Hills were the city walls; where the Senate's now fenced off,
    a warhorse drank from a bubbling spring.

Tatius barricaded the spring with a maple-wood stockade,
    encircling his camp for safety with piled-up earth.
A verdant copse was hidden in an ivy-covered glen,
    trees rustling to echo the natural waters,
the woodland home of Silvanus, where a shepherd's
                                        melodious pipe

called the ewes to drink, away from the heat.

Tarpeia had drawn fresh water for Vesta, carrying
    an urn of earthenware upon her head.
She saw Tatius exercising on the dusty plain,
    raising weapons sporting yellow plumes:
dumbfounded by the king's face and his regal armour,
    she let the urn slip through negligent hands.

Thereafter she blamed omens from the innocent moon
    for her need to go to the stream to wash her hair,
took silver lilies for the kindly nymphs, to have them
    shield Tatius' beauty from a Roman spear;
going back to the misty Capitol at the first smoke of evening,
    her arms were scratched by the trailing brambles;
resting in the citadel, she lamented suffering
    no neighbour of Jupiter should have to endure:

'Camp fires, staff headquarters of Tatius' battalions,
    Sabine armour that dazzles my eyes,
I wish that I could be a captive in your homeland,
    if I could only look at Tatius' face!
Goodbye Roman hills, and Rome cresting those hills,
    and Vesta, who'll blush at my wickedness:
that horse whose mane Tatius is dressing to the right,
    that horse will bring my love back to his camp.

'Why marvel that Scylla cut off her father's magic lock,
    her pale loins turned into savage dogs?
Or that Ariadne betrayed her monstrous horned brother,
    when the reeled-in thread found a way through the maze?
What infamy I'll bring on Italian girls, a servant
    picked for the virginal hearth gone to the bad!
If anyone's surprised that Minerva's fire has gone out,
    forgive me: it was my tears drenching her altar.

'Tomorrow, they say, there'll be drinking throughout the
                                        city: Tatius,
    take the spine of the thorny ridge at dawn.
The whole path is slippery and treacherous: the tricky
    route hides secret watercourses along it.
If only I knew the spells of magic incantations:
    my tongue, too, would then help my handsome hero.
A king's coloured toga would suit you – not that motherless
                                        child
    suckled on the hard teat of a wild she-wolf.

'Tell me, Tatius, shall I walk as a queen in your court?
    Rome betrayed is no mean dowry for you.
If not, let the Rape of the Sabine Women not go unpunished:
    take me: even the score by the law of reprisal.
As a bride, I can ease apart embattled infantry lines:
    so sign a treaty across my wedding dress.
Marriage god, play the music; bugler, stop those reveilles;
    believe it – my lovemaking will end your war.

'The horn is sounding the fourth watch and day's approach,
    the tired stars are dropping into the ocean.
I'll try to sleep; I hope that I will dream about you:
    bring your calming image before my eyes.'

She spoke and spread out her arms in an uneasy sleep,
    not knowing new demons lay in her embrace:
Venus, resolved to keep the Trojan embers glowing,
    fed her sin, spreading fire through her bones.
She raved like a bacchant beside the rushing Terme River,
    her clothes torn to expose her breasts.

The city held a *festa* – the Parilia, our fathers called it –
    marking the foundation of the walls,
an annual shepherds' junket, games all over town,

rustic trenchers dripping with plenty,
the tipsy crowd launching its grubby feet across
sacred heaps of blazing hay. Romulus
ordered the watch suspended to mark the holiday,
the barracks silent with no trumpet blare.

Tarpeia, thinking her time had come, went to meet the enemy:
she sealed the deal – her person part of it.
The hill, hard to climb, had been left free for the festival;
time pressed, barking dogs were put to the sword.
Sleep made a gift of everything, but Jupiter's will
was that she should stay awake for her punishment –
and could a single death suffice for the sinful girl
who wanted to betray the flame of Vesta?

She gave away the gate of Rome and the sleeping city
for a marriage day – any day he chose.
But Tatius was not a man to honour an act of treachery.
'Marry,' he said. 'Come to my kingdom's bed!'
He spoke, and he and his comrades crushed her under their
armour.
A dowry appropriate to her services.

So Jove's hill got its name of shame: wakeful Tarpeia,
you have your payback for your unjust lot.

IV.5

God rot you, madam,
and may the earth choke your grave with thorns,
your shade be in perpetual need of a drink,
your ghost have no rest when your body's ash,
and the hungry howl of vengeful Cerberus

terrorise your accursed bones.

You once could turn bashful Hippolytus
into a sexual predator,
doom the most harmonious union,
make Penelope jeer at talk
her husband's coming home, and bed
horny Antinous.
You said the word – magnets lost their pull,
mother birds became
*step*mothers to their nestlings.
You threw some graveyard herbs into
the irrigation channel –
standing crops were washed away by floods.
You could bewitch the moon,
make it dance to your song,
turn into a werewolf after sunset,
tear out ravens' eyes with your fingernails
to blind a husband watching for your tricks,
consult screech-owls about my blood-type,
and, to finish me off,
gather secretions from a mare in heat.

These were the words of your trade:
'You sexy girl, you make men hot:
let's have an eager crowd
beating the carriageway to your door.
You fancy gold and jewels from the East,
dresses with Tyrian dyes,
silks from Kos,
gilded Turkish bedspreads,
gifts from palm-fronded Egypt,
fluorspar cups from Persia ... ?
Then no more talk of faithfulness,
forget the gods, let lying reign supreme,

tear up the rules of chastity – it's too
expensive.

'Delays add value – fabricate excuses:
love put off just one night comes back stronger.
He messed your hair up? Anger pays:
he's under pressure when you trade for peace.
So now he's purchased sex, you've promised it –
tell him it's Isis time, so ten days off.
Let your maids harp on that it's April, and it's going
to be your birthday on the Ides of May.
Your suppliant's waiting; pull up a chair and write …
anything! If it scares him, you've got him.
Keep permanent love-bites around your neck
that he can think another man's teeth left.

'Don't take your cue from Medea's railing
(she put the question, so of course got dumped),
rather from suave Menander's pricy Thais,
when the comic harlot outwits cunning slaves.
Adapt to the style of your man: if he strikes up a tune,
drink with him and sing along.
Have the doorman check for gifts:
if an empty fist is knocking,
he can sleep on oblivious, head against the bolt.
It's a soldier, not exactly a Romeo,
or a horny-handed sailor? Don't turn him away
(if he's paying ready money);
ditto some barbarian who used to have
a label round his neck,
jumping about in the Forum on chalked feet.

'Keep your eyes on the gold, not the hand that brings it.
You hear poetry? What do you get aside from words?
If he's offering verses, but not clothes, from Kos,

say you can't hear him – till hard cash appears.
Make the best of the springtime of your youth,
the wrinkle-free age –
time won't make you any prettier.
I've seen rose gardens outstripping scented Paestum
wilt in a morning in the sirocco's breath.'

When Acanthis was drilling this into my lady-friend's head,
I was fast becoming skin and bones.
But now, Queen Venus, accept before your altar
the cut throat of a ring-dove for grace received:
I saw a rattling cough
take hold in her wrinkled neck,
bloody spit ooze out between
her cavity-filled teeth,
and her putrid soul expire
into her ancient mattress:
her sagging hovel shivered as the fire died.
For her funeral she can have
the stolen bands around her scanty hair,
her cap discoloured by the filth of neglect,
and the dog that was only too wakeful – to my cost –
when my thumb was about to slip the lock.
An old, broken-necked amphora can be
the madam's tomb:
fig tree, squeeze your roots, vice-like, about it.

And lovers, pelt this grave with sharp-edged stones;
add curses to those rocks to crush her bones.

IV.6

The bard is beginning the rites. Silence, please.
One blow to fell the heifer at my altar.
A Roman garland to rival Philitas' ivy,
a jug to pour Cyrenean water.
Give me soft spikenard, offerings of seductive
incense, wind wool three times round the altar.
Sprinkle me with water, have the ivory flute
pour a libation of song from Turkish jars.
Away with dishonesty, let all evil seek
some other sky: pure laurel smooths the bard's new path.

Muse, we shall tell of Apollo's Palatine home,
a theme, Calliope, that deserves your blessing.
These are songs to the greater glory of Caesar; when Caesar
is sung, even Jupiter must pay attention.

Apollo's port pushes into Epirus,
a bay buries Ionian breakers' rumble;
Roman ships mass at Actium's memorials;
the sea now beset by sailors' supplications.
Here the world's forces forgathered, a fir forest's
vast volume in the waves, but omens uneven:
one rank relegated to ruin by Romulus,
with weapons wielded, shamefully, by a woman;
facing – Augustus' fleet, sails filled with Jove's afflatus,
its standards long skilled to strike for the nation.

The combat lines were curved in a couple of crescents,
the sheen of weapons wavering on the water,
as Apollo, leaving his Delos to lie motionless
(once it had floated, just a toy of the tempest),
perched over Augustus' prow, and a pulse
of fire flashed three times in a zigzag fork.

Now his hair did not hang down his shoulders,
no leisurely lay from a lyre of tortoiseshell,
rather the glower he gave Agamemnon,
gutting the Greek camp for the greedy pyre,
or when he slew the sinuous Python serpent,
the monster menacing the gentle Muses.

He said: 'World-saver, son of Alba Longa,
Augustus, more acclaimed than Trojan ancestors,
you control the land — conquer at sea; for your cause
my bow battles, and my back's arrow burden.
Free the nation from fear; its folk have faith in you,
piling your ship with the public prayers;
if you do not defend it, Romulus did not
auspiciously view twelve vultures over the Palatine.

'Enemy oars approach too close: a catastrophe
that Roman waves carry a queen's sails while you command.
There's nothing to fear if their fleet coming forward
has hundred-oared warships: the sea holds them back;
and those timbers that threaten with rock-throwing Centaurs
are nothing but hollow planks whose power is paint.
It's the cause that makes or breaks courage in a soldier —
if it's not just, the disgrace disarms him.
Time now: engage, and I, who have set the time,
will convey the Julian vessels to victory.'

He had ended, and emptied his quiverful on the enemy;
after those bowshots Caesar's spear came second.
Rome's faith in Phoebus triumphs; the female is punished,
her shattered sceptre tossed by Ionian waves.
And Julius stared down in astonishment from his star:
'No one can deny our bloodline's divinity.'
Triton's horn hailed the homecoming, all the goddesses
of the sea clapped hands, saluting freedom's standards.

But She heads to hide in the Nile in her fugitive
felucca – she won't die on a day that's demanded.
All the better! A tiny triumph one woman would be,
led through the lanes Jugurtha trod long ago!
Apollo's Actium memorials were made because
every shaft he shot subdued ten ships.

Done – my war poem! Victorious Apollo's requesting
the lute, stripping off his armour for peaceful dancing.
Party-time in white clothes in the shaded grove:
I'll have scented roses round my neck,
flowing wine squeezed from Falernian presses,
Cilician fragrance sprayed on my hair.

Poets need a drink for the Muse to stir their talent:
Bacchus, you usually inspire your brother Apollo.
One scribe can record the defeat of marsh-dwelling
                                        Rhinelanders,
another versify Ethiopia's dark kingdom;
a third report the late treaty to deal with the Parthians:
'They can give back Rome's standards – soon we'll be taking
                                        theirs;
generous Augustus is sparing the Easterners' arrows,
but he's just deferring the trophies for his offspring.
Good news, Crassus, if you feel anything out there
in the sand – we can cross the Euphrates to visit your tomb!'

Wine and song is how I'll pass my nights,
until day casts its rays into my cup.

IV.7

Ghosts exist then: death doesn't end it all;
the pallid shade eludes the guttering pyre.
Cynthia, just buried to the trumpet's knell,
leaned across my bed, I thought,
when fitful sleep after her funeral
dipped to the chilly empire of my sheets.
Her hair the same as when they took her away,
her eyes the same, her dress scorched on one side,
fire-marks on the familiar beryl ring,
her lips worn down by Lethe's water,
she summoned living breath and voice, snapping
the thumb and fingers of her brittle hand:

'Traitor, no girl can hope for much from you!
Nodding off already? Forgotten
our assignations in Subura? No sleep then!
Those night escapades that grooved my window-sill?
I slipped out often, swinging down a rope
hand over hand into your arms.
We made love by the corner, chest to chest,
our clinches warming up the city street.
So much, then, for your promises: just words
stripped away by the unhearing winds.

'No one cried out at my passing –
your voice might have secured one day's reprieve.
No undertaker even hired; a broken
tile gashed my unprotected head.
Who saw you, at my funeral, hunched in grief?
Was your coat warm with tears? Did you wear black?
Too far to trail my cortege all the way?
You could have ordered it to move more slowly.
No prayers were heard from you for winds to stoke

my flames, no fragrance sweetened up the fire.
Would some cheap hyacinths have left you broke?
Or a wine flagon cost too much to crack?

'Put Lygdamus on the rack; heat up the steel:
I knew his tricks when I drank that cloudy wine;
cunning Nomas may hide her brews –
a touch of fire will soon make her confess!
Some tart once offering a cut-price night
paces your floor now in a gold-trimmed dress;
if my complexion's praised by servant girls,
they'll soon get mounds of wool to spin;
old Petale, who took wreaths to my tomb,
was clamped in horrid shackles. Lalage
was thrashed, suspended by her curls,
for asking just one favour in my name.
You let your new love melt my statuette
so she could pay her dowry from the gold.

'Guilty as charged, Propertius –
but I won't hound you.
I ruled your books – you gave me a long run.
I swear by the Fates, whose thread can't be unspun,
and so may Cerberus let me quietly past,
that I was loyal. May a snake twist round
my bones, hissing in my grave, if I lie.

'The river of death has two destinations;
departed souls row one way or the other.
For Clytemnestra and Pasiphae (she
who built the monstrous wooden cow) the boat
goes hellwards; flower-decked craft take others
where the wind caresses Elysian roses,
where sweet-toned lutes, Cybele's cymbals
and Eastern lyres of turbaned troupes keep time.

Andromeda and Hypermnestra, wives
of virtue, tell the stories of their vows.
The first recounts how chains caused by her mother
bruised her on cold rocks where her arms were pinned;
the second how her sisters planned a crime
but she recoiled at the atrocity.
With tears in death we seal love in our lives;
your many infidelities I pass over.

'Now your instructions – if you're so inclined,
and Chloris' herbs haven't got you in their grip.
Look after Parthenie, my nurse,
in her old age; she was always kind to you;
and don't make Latris, my favourite maid,
hold up the mirror for a new mistress;
any last poems you've written about me –
burn them: don't keep my praises in your drawer.
Plant ivy on my tomb, its swelling fruit
and tendrils twining round my bones.
Where the Aniene floods the orchards,
and ivory, thanks to Hercules, stays white,
carve this fitting verse upon a stone,
brief words for the commuter out of Rome:

IN TIVOLI'S SOIL HERE GOLDEN CYNTHIA LIES,
FOR SWEET ANIENE'S BANKS AN ADDED PRIZE.

'Don't spurn the dreams that come from paradise:
righteous visions possess the weight of truth.
At night we roam, night frees the imprisoned dead,
even Cerberus strays, the bolt slides from the gate.
Laws send us back to Lethe at daybreak:
we board, the boatman counts his cargo.

'Have other women now, you're theirs to take:

you'll soon be mine, our bones will grind as one.'

At last her long complaint at me was done:
her wraith escaped my outstretched arms and fled.

IV.8

READ ALL ABOUT IT! MAJOR RIOT ON ESQUILINE!
LOCAL RESIDENTS TAKE REFUGE IN NEW PARK!

* * * * *

Lanuvio, long the home of a patron snake,
is worth a detour for an hour or so.
Where a dark cleft bisects a steep ravine,
a virgin must go, by an old custom,
to feed the hungry serpent when he demands
his annual meal, hissing from the depths.
Girls sent for that ritual turn pale
when their soft hands stray near the reptile's jaws.
He grabs the food the maiden proffers,
the basket trembling in her grasp.
If she's been good, she'll make it safely home;
farmers will cry: 'A bumper crop this year!'

There Cynthia travelled by pony and trap
to worship Juno (or Venus, more likely),
her progress witnessed by the Appian Way,
whose paving stones her coach-wheels rattled over.
She looked a sight, bent forward with the reins,
provoking ribald jokes about her driving.
(The less said the better about her smooth-chinned beau,
his swerving carriage and dogs with fancy collars.

Let's hope he'll end up as a gladiator,
unable to afford a razor blade.)

With Cynthia cheating on me again, I vowed
to pitch my camp-bed elsewhere. On the Aventine
a certain Phyllis lives (when sober, boring;
a pleasure drunk). Below the Capitol
there's another, Teia, pretty but
a man-eater in her cups. I invited both
to sweeten up my night and boost
my love-life, sampling pastures new. One couch
for three, a garden screened from view.
Seating arrangements? Me between the two.
Lygdamus was our *sommelier* and got
the summer glassware out and best Greek wine.
A flute-player from Egypt, Syrian castanets,
fresh rose-petals ready to strew, and Magnus,
more skilful than his shrunken frame suggests,
gyrated his stunted forearms to the tune.

The lamps were full – yet flickered constantly;
the table collapsed, another ominous sign.
I played at dice, hoping that full houses
would spur libido; ones was all I threw.
I ignored the girls' songs (and unbuttoned blouses):
Lanuvio's gate danced before my eyes.
Then suddenly the creak of hinges,
the sound of voices in the alleyway.

In seconds, Cynthia burst into the place,
her hair undone, but radiant in her fury.
My wine-glass slipped out of my nerveless fingers;
sozzled, I couldn't move my pallid lips.
Her eyes, in womanly rage, darted lightning
in a scene reminiscent of the sack of Troy.

She sank her talons into Phyllis' face.
'Help!' Teia called out. 'Neighbours, there's a fire!'
The shouting woke the Romans from their dreams,
the whole street echoed with the angry screams.
The girls, their hair torn and their clothes awry,
took refuge in the nearest bar in town.

Pumped up with victory, Cynthia tracked me down,
swung a back-hander that left my nose bloody,
planted a line of tooth-marks round my neck,
and blackened with great care each guilty eye.
The fun of hitting me now wearing thin,
Lygdamus was dragged from where he hid behind
the couch, pleading with me to save his skin.
I was a prisoner just like you were, buddy.

I reached out in unconditional surrender.
Cynthia allowed me just to touch her toe,
saying: 'If you wish me to forgive your sin,
accept my terms, which are as follows:
1) No more going to Pompey's Portico
or the Forum seeking friends of female gender;
2) Don't crane round for girls in the back row
at plays, or ogle them as they drive past;
3) Lygdamus, the cause of all my troubles,
must go on sale, his ankles clapped in irons.'

Those were her terms. I answered: 'Yes, of course.'
She laughed for all to hear. She had her way.
The doorstep that the girls had crossed to come
she scrubbed, and all the rooms she fumigated.
She made me put new oil in all the lamps
and dabbed hot sulphur three times on my head.
A change of sheets – the deal was consummated.

Cynthia and I made peace, all over the bed.

IV.9

When Hercules drove the bullocks from the stalls of Erythea,
he came to the sheep-grazed Palatine, the unconquerable heights,
and stopped the cattle there (they were tired; he was tired),
where the Velabro formed a pool of river water
and boatmen steered their craft where city streets now run.
But they weren't safe: Cacus proved a deceitful host
and stole the oxen, contravening Jupiter's law.
Cacus was a local, a bandit who lived in a menacing cave,
the sounds he uttered divided between his triple mouths.
To try to disguise the blatant evidence of his theft,
he dragged the cattle backwards by their tails into his cave.

But he could not fool Hercules; the bullocks lowed,
and our hero trashed the robber's horrible home in a rage.
Cacus lay dead, his three heads smashed by the famous cudgel;
Hercules said: 'Let's go, cattle – you were my club's last labour:
twice I sought you out, and twice you were my reward;
go and name these fields with your bovine lowing: one day
your pasture will be Rome's renowned Forum Bovarium.'

But now a thirst tormented Hercules' dry throat,
and the land, though fertile, offered no source of fresh water;
in the distance he heard the laughter of girls in an enclosure,
where a circular wall hemmed in a shaded grove,
the sealed-off place of the women's goddess, venerable springs,
and rites that no man ever saw without punishment.
Crimson ribbons covered a secluded doorway
where a ramshackle cottage glowed with scented flames,
a poplar adorned the shrine with its grey-green leaves,
birdsong was hidden somewhere in a mass of shade.

Hercules raced here, dust caking his dry beard,
uttering less than god-like words outside the door:

'Whoever you are who frolic in the sacred bower, please,
open your sanctuary to welcome a worn-out man.
I've been wandering round in need, I can hear spring-water
                                        sounding,
just what cupped hands could take from a stream would be
                                        enough.
Did you ever hear of someone who propped up the globe on
                                        his back?
I'm him: the world I took on my shoulders calls me Alcides.
Who doesn't know about the exploits of Hercules' club,
the arrows that never missed against notorious monsters?
The one man who turned on the lights down in the Stygian
                                        gloom?

Now I've arrived in this corner of Earth, but my travails
go on: I'm exhausted but no roof is open to me.
Even if you were performing rites for spiteful Juno,
she would not have refused me water – and she's my
                                        stepmother!
Maybe it's my face or my lion's mane that frightens
you all, or else my hair, scorched by the Libyan sun,
but once I did household tasks, dressed in a purple gown,
and completed a daily assignment of spinning in Lydia;
a breast-band of soft cloth covered the hair on my chest
and despite my calloused hands I made a convincing girl.'

Hercules' argument; but the gracious priestess, whose white
hair was bound with a scarlet ribbon, answered him:
'Don't damage your eyes, my friend; this grove is dangerous:
leave now – get away from the doorway while the going's good.
The altar that's protected by the loneliness of this cottage
is closed to men and avenged by an implacable law.
The prophet Tiresias paid a high price for seeing Minerva
when she put down the Gorgon's head and bathed her strong
                                        limbs.

I hope you find other springs: this water's reserved for women,
a private stream that flows along a secret course.'

But Hercules put his shoulder to that shaded entrance
and the door could not withstand a fury driven by thirst.
When he had drained the stream and slaked his burning throat,
his lips barely dry, he pronounced this fateful sentence:
'The Ara Maxima, vowed when I recovered my cattle,
the biggest altar these hands ever built,' (he said),
'will never be opened up for veneration by women;
so may the thirst be avenged of Hercules the traveller.'
And since he had sanctified a world cleansed by his hands,
the Sabine town of Cures worshipped him as Sancus.
Lord Hercules, whom stern Juno now smiles on, I greet you;
Sancus, be present in my book and bless it.

IV.10

And now: the origins of Feretrian Jupiter
and how three sets of weapons were taken from three leaders.
It's a stiff climb, but one powered by hopes of glory:
garlands from easily reached flowers are not for me.

Romulus set the precedent for this award,
coming back from the enemy laden with rewards,
when his spear killed Acron the Sabine in front
of our gates, felling him upon his toppled mount.
Acron, son of Hercules, commander from the city
of Caenina, had threatened Roman territory.
He had dared to hope for spoils from Romulus' body,
but ended up yielding his own, wet and bloody.
Romulus had seen him outside the city's cavernous towers,
armed to the teeth, but got in with a quickly answered vow:

'Jupiter, Acron will fall today as an offering to you.'
His enemy fell, a spoil to Jove – the vow came true.
Another victory for our nation's valorous father,
schooled in a humble home to endure martial rigour.
The same horse served for war or else to go ploughing;
a shaggy crest decked out his helmet of wolf skin.
His painted shield had no inlay of glittering gilt,
and slaughtered oxen furnished a durable sword-belt.

Next in line was Cossus, who killed the Veian Tolumnius,
when defeating Veii was a challenge for Rome.
War clamour had not crossed the Tiber: Nomentum's conquest
and Cora's, with its three acres per settler, were our furthest.
Alas poor Veii, in time past you too were a kingdom
and a gilded chair was set out in your forum;
now the wandering shepherd's horn sounds alone
inside your walls and ploughs turn up the occasional bone.
The Veiian chief was perched on the tower above his gates
seeking talks with the enemy, trusting in his wits;
the battering ram was pounding the wall with its bronze head,
a long mantlet shielding the siege work that had started,
when Cossus said: 'Brave men should fight out in the open.'
No sooner said than done: each man stood on the plain.
Rome had God on its side that day, and Tolumnius'
severed neck splashed with blood the Roman horses.

Claudius beat off the enemies who had crossed the Po,
bringing home the Belgian shield of the giant who
led them, Virdomarus. He claimed descent from Brennus,
and his shower of javelins from the front chariot was famous.
But the twisted torque fell from his sliced throat
and he stained his striped breeches with his blood.

Now trophies from all three are stored in the temple; Feretrian
means leader struck – *ferit* – leader, confident in the omens,

or that they brought back — *ferebant* — the arms on their
                                        shoulders;
and hence the proud altar is called Feretrian Jupiter's.

IV.11

Paullus, desist. Spare my tomb further tears.
The black gate will not swing wide at your prayers;
the dead, once subject to the next world's code,
find solid steel paving a one-way road.
The master of these dark halls may hear the sound,
but all your weeping soaks into deaf ground.
Though gods like offerings, once the boatman's paid,
mean-spirited fate seals off the world of shade.
The trumpets wailed enough when the torch fire
was lit to take me from the funeral pyre.
My glittering marriage, ancient family tree,
loyal child-bearing, were no help to me.
Was fate less hostile to Cornelia?
Five fingers easily now encompass her.

Slow tide of Acheron in night's endless seat,
whatever waters swirl about my feet,
I come here free of guilt, early at most,
and ask no special lenience for my ghost;
if Aeacus sits as judge beside the urn,
let him assess my case when it's my turn;
his brothers too, and next to Minos' chair
the band of Furies in the court's still air.
Sisyphus, leave that rock; let Ixion's wheel
be still and Tantalus' water mirage real,
villainous Cerberus chase no shades today,
his chain hang slack, the door-bar pushed away.

I'll plead my own defence and if it fails,
like Danaus' daughters, carry leaky pails.

Can spoils of warfare won by ancestors
prove virtue? Spanish bronze entered our doors;
my mother's side is no less marked by fame,
each house has special honours to its name.
I cast no smear on my forefathers' slate;
I was a model others emulate.
My girlish frocks gave way to wedding dresses,
a married woman's headband tied my tresses;
I slept in Paullus' bed and my gravestone
proclaims I was the bride of him alone.

Two public posts my brother occupied;
his consul year triumphant – but I died.
By my forebears our city glorifies,
and under whose flag shattered Carthage lies,
and who destroyed the king of Macedon
boasting of being Achilles' distant son –
I swear I never broke the laws of Rome
or through my conduct stained our family home.

And nothing changed, innocence marked it all:
a radiant path, marriage to funeral.
Bloodlines dictated how I led my life;
no judge's frown could make a better wife.
Though judgement passed on me might be severe,
my presence gives no woman cause for fear:
not matchless Claudia, who with a cord
moved the stuck ship with Cybele aboard,
not chaste Aemilia, who saved Vesta's fire,
her linen robe making the flame blaze higher.
I brought no shame upon you, darling mother:
nothing (but death) would you wish any other.

Civic laments are added to your moans,
even Caesar weeps to vindicate my bones.
His daughter's worthy sister was laid low,
the emperor grieves – we saw a god's tears flow.

I earned the garments of a fruitful spouse,
and was not stolen from a barren house.
All's well: I never mourned a child's decease;
they all survived to see me rest in peace.
My sons, my consolation since I passed,
it was your hands that closed my eyes at last.
Daughter, whose birth enhanced your father's bid
for office, wed once, as your mother did.
That is the high point of a woman's glory
when people praise her married life's full story.
All, multiply, and if our line pursues
my deeds, I gladly take death's final cruise.

Paullus, to you our children I bequeath:
my body is ashes, but such cares still breathe.
Be mother and father now; as they grow older
their full weight comes to rest upon your shoulder.
Add my kisses to yours to staunch their weeping:
all our household will be in your safe-keeping.
Don't grieve yourself while they are standing by,
and when they come, make sure your cheeks are dry.
Night is appointed for your hopeless yearning,
seeing my shape in dreams, tossing and turning.
When talking to a picture of my face
in secret, for an answer leave a space.

But should a new stepmother then be wed,
nervously sitting on the marriage bed,
then greet your father's union with praise,
children, and captivate her with your ways;

don't laud your mother, lest comparison sparks
affronts to her from casual remarks.
If, for your father, memory should suffice,
putting on my remains so high a price,
learn to allay the old age that arrives,
those trials that descend on widowers' lives.
May all those years I lost be given to you,
so that my offspring grant him joy anew.

I rest my case; sad witnesses, please stand;
Earth, pay rewards my virtues now demand.
Goodness has opened heaven; may I be found
worthy to sail where honoured souls are bound.

NOTES

Notes to the Poems

I.1

Aspects of the poem are discussed in the introduction.

Tullus: A friend and possible early patron of Propertius. He is commonly identified as the nephew of Lucius Volcacius Tullus, a prominent Roman politician. Other poems are also addressed to him, including 1.6 (qv).

Milanion: In Greek mythology, one of several names cited as the successful suitor of Atalanta, a princess who was exposed to die as a newborn because she was not a male heir. She was nursed by a bear, and later brought up by hunters, becoming herself a hunter before finding her way back home. Propertius relates how Milanion wooed her, enduring hardships for her in the fastnesses of Arcadia, including a bruising encounter with a Centaur (half-man, half-horse). He makes only a glancing reference to the best-known version of the story in which Atalanta, who excels at running, challenges suitors to a race: the first man to beat her can marry her, but those who lose are put to death. Milanion defeats her by dropping golden apples, given to him by Venus, in her path; these cause Atalanta to slow down, as she stops to pick them up.

I.2

Outfit from Kos: The eastern Mediterranean island was famed for its diaphanous fabrics.

Leucippus' daughters: Phoebe and Helaira, Greek mythological sisters who were carried off by the twins Castor and Pollux (later becoming the constellation Gemini) despite being betrothed to other men. **Marpessa** attracted two suitors, the god Apollo and the mortal Idas. Jupiter, the king of the gods, ruled that she should choose between them and she opted for Idas on the grounds that he would grow old with her.

Hippodamia: Daughter of the mythological King Oenomaus of Elis, who forced all applicants for her hand to compete with him in a chariot race, on pain of death if they lost. But Pelops, from Phrygia in Asia Minor, had a servant of Oenomaus sabotage his master's chariot, causing a fatal crash and enabling him to marry Hippodamia.

Apelles: A renowned fourth-century-BC Greek artist; originally from Colophon, he died in Kos.

Calliope: One of the Muses.

Minerva and Venus: Cynthia possessed the practical skills associated with the former and the good looks dear to the latter.

Ariadne: Lovers of Richard Strauss' opera *Ariadne auf Naxos* will be familiar with the story of the Cretan princess who helped the Athenian hero Theseus slay the Minotaur, a monster that was half man, half bull. Theseus took her with him as he journeyed back to Athens but abandoned her as she slept on the island of Naxos.

Andromeda: The daughter of an Ethiopian king, who chained her to a rock as an offering to placate a ravening sea-monster, sent by the sea-god Neptune to punish her mother's boast of being more beautiful than sea-nymphs. She was rescued and married by Perseus.

Thracian maenad: Maenads were devotees of the wine-god Dionysus (Bacchus to the Romans), whose ecstatic worship was said to be widespread in Thrace, northeast Greece.

Argus: Io was one of many mortal women loved by Jupiter. When his wife Juno accused him of adultery, he denied it and turned Io into a cow. Juno (who in another version was the one who gave Io bovine form) appointed the giant Argus as a sentinel to keep watch on her; his hundred eyes meant that he was ever-watchful.

I.4

Bassus: According to Ovid, a writer of 'iambics' (often verse lampoons).

Antiope ... Hermione: Two relatively minor figures chosen as examples of Greek mythological beauties. Antiope (see also note to III.15) was one of Jupiter's paramours. Hermione was the daughter of Helen of Troy and her husband Menelaus, king of Sparta.

I.5

Gallus: Propertius discloses the name of the addressee only at the end of the poem, but I have brought it up to the beginning to help the modern reader. The same name occurs in other poems in Book One. On the basis of the reference in this poem to aristocratic ancestry (Latin '*nobilitas*'), many scholars have argued that it cannot be the poet-politician Cornelius Gallus, who served in Egypt but fell foul of Augustus and committed suicide in 27 or 26 BC. That Gallus came from provincial stock. But Francis Cairns has made a case that Propertius is addressing his fellow poet, who also crops up in Vergil's *Eclogues*. Gallus, of whose work only a handful of fragments survives, is credited with having pioneered the writing of love poetry in elegiac couplets in Latin, and hence was important to Propertius; the identification of the supposed originator of a genre was commonplace in

Greek and Latin literature. The present poem, in which Propertius teases Gallus over his supposed desire to start a relationship with Cynthia, has an obvious parallel with the preceding one, in which he humorously takes to task another poet, Bassus, for trying to get him to drop Cynthia. The *nobilitas* argument does not seem conclusive as Gallus may have come from a prominent provincial family.

Thessaly: This part of Greece had a reputation for witches and magic.

I.6

Tullus: See note to I.1. The present poem has some foundation in historical fact, in that Tullus' uncle was appointed proconsul of 'Asia' – what we would now call Asia Minor, i.e. part of Turkey. Propertius appears to say his friend is going there in an advance party and has invited the poet to accompany him. Such assignments were common career moves for young men of Propertius' social class, but we have no independent evidence of it. In any case the situation provides an occasion for a typical Propertian motif – that he has no talent for warfare, and prefers the *militia amoris*, or service of love. 'The cherub' refers to the love-god.

Ionia: The western seaboard of Turkey, whose cities were Greek in ancient times. The River **Pactolus** was famed for its deposits of gold, or rather electrum (an alloy of gold and silver), which enabled the state of Lydia, where it was located, to create some of the earliest coinage. It is thought to be what is now called in Turkish the Sart Çayı, a tributary of the River Gediz.

I.7

Ponticus: An epic poet of the day, also mentioned by Ovid. History was not kind to his work, none of which has survived, as Propertius perhaps foresees in this first skirmish with those who think he too should be writing epic, not love lyrics. Ponticus was evidently working on a poem about the war of succession in mythical Thebes, in which Oedipus' sons, Eteocles and Polynices, fought over the throne. The reference later in Propertius' poem to seven armies refers to the allies recruited by Polynices to try to oust his brother, as immortalised in Aeschylus' play, *Seven Against Thebes*.

The Lad: Cupid.

I.8a

Propertius' version of a genre of classical poetry known by the Greek word *propemptikon*, or farewell to a departing friend. In the medieval manuscripts, what are here printed as 1.8a and 1.8b appear as a single poem, but most modern editors split it in two. In either case, 8a is clearly a set-up for 8b, in which Propertius exults that Cynthia has decided not to leave after all but to stay with him.

The freezing Balkans: The Roman province known then as Illyricum – broadly, parts of the Dalmatian coast. This poem, like several others, paints a picture of Cynthia making her living by sleeping with wealthy men – often, as suggested here, government officials on foreign postings. Poem II.16a also talks of a governor returning from Illyricum and being a likely client of Cynthia, leading some editors to conjecture that the same man is referred to here. None of this is to be taken too literally. The hardships Cynthia will supposedly endure if she goes to Illyricum with 'Mr. What's-his-name' are literary/rhetorical rather than realistic.

The Pleiades: The constellation whose rise in the spring marked the beginning of the sailing season.

Karaburun: A long peninsula in what is now southern Albania, directly across the Strait of Otranto from Italy, and known to the ancients as Ceraunia. Its rocks were a formidable shipping hazard. Orikum (ancient Oricos) is a port at the southern end of the Bay of Vlorë.

Jason and the Argonauts: I have followed Heyworth's suggestion that the obscure and probably corrupt place-names given in the manuscripts in fact refer to stopping points on the outward and return journeys of the Argonauts, who sailed to Colchis (in what is now Georgia) in search of the Golden Fleece.

I.8b

Elis ... Hippodamia: See note to 1.2. The implication here is evidently that the unsuccessful suitors had forfeited their wealth to Elis, making it rich.

I.9

Ponticus: The epic poet already addressed in 1.7, to which this poem is a sequel. Or rather, 1.7 is a set-up for this poem (told you so!).

Dodona's prophetic pigeons: Doves at a famous oracle of Jupiter at Dodona in Epirus, north-west Greece.

Thebes' lyre-built ramparts: According to myth, the lyre-playing of Amphion was so sweet it enticed the stones to slide into place to construct the walls of Thebes, the city whose story is the theme of Ponticus' epic.

Mimnermus: A seventh-century-BC Greek love poet from Smyrna (now Izmir) in Asia Minor; he was later claimed by the people of Colophon. A few of his poems survive, written in elegiac couplets, the metre used by Propertius.

Strapped to a wheel: The punishment of Ixion in the underworld for attempting to seduce Juno, wife of Jupiter.

I.10

Gallus: See note to I.5.

I.11

Baia: A fashionable seaside resort at the west end of the Gulf of Naples. Ancient Rome's equivalent of St Tropez, it had a similar reputation for holiday romances.

Hercules' causeway: A coastal path in the area, supposedly built by the legendary hero. It passed between the small Lake Lucrino (mentioned later on) and the sea.

Admire how the sea...: The obscure text in the manuscripts has been argued over by scholars. I have paraphrased to adopt the least improbable suggestion of a reference to the construction in 37 BC by Octavian's right-hand man Agrippa of a channel linking the sea to Lake Lucrino and then further inland to Lake Averno, in order to create a port (the Portus Iulius) to provide safe harbour for the future emperor's fleet in his campaign against Sextus Pompeius (son of Pompey the Great and the last major rallying-point for opposition against the Second Triumvirate).

Cuma: A town near Baia.

I.12

The Volga: The Hypanis, referred to in the Latin, is sometimes identified with what is now the Bug, which flows through Ukraine and Poland. Propertius certainly knew next to nothing about rivers in this area, and I have substituted the Volga on grounds of both familiarity (for the modern reader) and cadence. Both are far from Italy.

Some oriental herb: The ancients believed that herbal brews could either inspire or chill amorous feelings.

I.13

Gallus: See note to I.5.

You outstripped Neptune...: I have simplified the complex mythology here. Tyro fell in love with the river-god Enipeus in Thessaly, northern Greece. Neptune, who lusted after Tyro, disguised himself as the river in order to possess her. Hercules ended his mortal existence on a pyre on Mount Oeta in Greece and was promptly deified, marrying Hebe, goddess of youth and cup-bearer to the gods, once he reached Olympus.

Leda: Wife of King Tyndareus of Sparta, she was seduced by Jupiter disguised as a swan, as in W. B. Yeats' famous poem. She gave birth to Helen (of Troy) and Clytemnestra, whom Agamemnon took as his wife and queen.

I.14

I think of you: See also the notes to 1.1 and 1.6 on Tullus. The opening lines depict the wealthy young man in his Tiber-side villa, complete with carefully planted park. Despite the 'money can't buy me love' message, Propertius laments elsewhere that money *can* buy the love – or at least the body – of Cynthia.

Rivers of Asia: Another reference to the Pactolus – see note to 1.6.

Carrara marble: The Latin text says 'an Arabian threshold'. Arabia was thought to be the source of onyx, an expensive kind of marble. I have substituted the better known Carrara marble, and 'cloth of gold' for the 'purple' (designating luxury) of the original.

Alcinous: A king who, in Homer's *Odyssey*, bestowed rich gifts on Odysseus (Ulysses). He was also famed for the wealth of his gardens, so there may be a reference back to Tullus' parklands.

I.15

Danger: Propertius does not spell out the danger he claims he was in. It is doubtless fictitious, though literal-minded commentators have speculated that he was on a risky voyage (but then how could Cynthia visit him?) or was ill. In practice, it simply provides the argument: Cynthia has failed to match the devotion of Greek mythological heroines.

Calypso: In the *Odyssey*, Ulysses dallied with the nymph Calypso on her Mediterranean island before resuming his voyage back home to Ithaca from the Trojan War.

Hypsipyle: A princess on the Aegean island of Lemnos who entertained Jason (from Thessaly on the Greek mainland) during his quest for the Golden Fleece.

Evadne: Wife of the Greek mythological warrior Capaneus, she threw herself on his funeral pyre after he was killed. Capaneus was one of the 'Seven Against Thebes' (see note to 1.7). He did not die at the hands of enemies but was struck down by Zeus (Jupiter) for blasphemy; he features in Dante's *Inferno*.

I.16

A door: This poem is a variant on a staple of ancient Greek and Latin literature, the *paraklausithyron*, or utterance by a lover outside the locked door of his beloved. In some cases the *'exclusus amator'* addresses the beloved; here the narrator is the door, but the bulk of the poem consists of a tirade by the lover against the door. We are left in the dark as to whether the resident female is meant to be a prostitute, the mistress of a wealthy man, or simply a woman who sleeps around. Propertius' stab at the genre bears some similarities to Catullus' Poem 67, couched as a dialogue between himself and a door, in which the house's decline from a grand past to a sordid present is likewise lamented. Here, it is not stated that the woman is Cynthia or that the lover is Propertius (although he does say he writes fashionable poetry); that the poem is about Cynthia would not have been lost on readers – the omission of her name from poems concerning her is not at all unusual in Propertius' work.

The goddess of chastity: Following Heyworth's acceptance of an emendation to the obscure manuscript text to give a reference to *Patricia Pudicitia*, chastity personified as a goddess, whose statue stood in the Roman Forum.

I.17

Cassiope's setting: Following the Oxford Classical Text reading, referring to the myth of Cassiope, whose arrogance led to her daughter Andromeda being offered as a victim to a marauding sea-monster (see note to 1.3). Both women ended up as constellations. As with the later mention of the Gemini, Propertius is looking – as the ancients habitually did – to the stars to change the weather and allow him to sail home. A variant reading, taking Cassiope to be a small port of that name on the Greek island of Corfu, would have Propertius still at sea. But the rest of the poem suggests he is on land, marooned by storms in a remote location after setting off on his travels. Either way, we are surely dealing as often with a dramatic scenario, not a real event. As in several other poems, Propertius switches between second and third person references to Cynthia. The Italian poet Ugo Foscolo imitated the start of this piece in a sonnet.

Gemini: Castor and Pollux were patrons of mariners.

Daughters of the princess of the ocean: The fifty sea-nymphs known as Nereids, daughters of Nereus and Doris (herself the daughter of the marine deity Oceanus).

I.18

Pan: A Greek rural god. He pursued the wood-nymph Pitys, who only eluded him by being changed into a fir tree. The beech may be mentioned because its smooth bark lends itself (even today) to the carving of amorous messages.

I.19

Protesilaus: The first Greek warrior to fall before the walls of Troy. On hearing of his death, his wife Laodamia persuaded the gods to let his shade pay her a brief visit, after which she committed suicide.

While we can...: Perhaps an echo of Catullus' celebrated Poem 5: 'Lesbia live with me / & love me ... / This sun once set / will rise again, / when our sun sets / follows night & / an endless sleep.' (Peter Whigham's translation).

I.20

Gallus: See note to 1.5. This time it's a boy that Gallus has fallen in love with.

Argonauts: See note to 1.8a. Hercules was one of Jason's team. The story of him losing his beloved Hylas to the nymphs was familiar to Propertius' readers from Hellenistic versions, by Theocritus and Apollonius Rhodius in particular. The ironic twist the poet gives is a warning that Gallus' Hylas is so beautiful he might be snatched away by latter-day 'nymphs' – the young women of contemporary Rome.

River Ascanius: The action takes place in Mysia, part of what is now northwest Turkey, but the River Ascanius and Mount Arganthus, mentioned later, cannot be identified.

Aniene: The ancient Anio, a picturesque small river flowing through Tivoli, east of Rome.

I.21

In this variant on the common classical theme of a tomb inscription addressing the passer-by, the speaker is a soldier who was a victim of the siege of Perugia in 41–40 BC by the forces of Octavian. The revolt at Perugia, led by Mark Antony's brother Lucius, may have been partly intended to weaken Octavian. It seems likely that the speaker is the relative of Propertius mentioned in the next poem, who died in the siege but whose body was never recovered. The person addressed is an imaginary fellow soldier fleeing the scene.

I eluded...: The manuscripts name the speaker as Gallus, but I incline to Heyworth's view that this is a copyist's error, representing a 'leakage' from the previous poem. Otherwise we have a puzzling confusion with the Gallus who figures in four other poems in Book One, and who may well be the soldier-poet of that name. I have therefore omitted it. I have also omitted the name Acca for the speaker's sister, which is itself a conjecture.

I.22

Perugia: Today the Umbrian capital, but once an Etruscan city. See note to previous poem. Perugia is just a few miles from Propertius' presumed birthplace of Assisi.

II.1

Silk from Kos: See note to I.2.

Maecenas: With Book Two, Propertius for the first time addresses Maecenas, perhaps the most famous literary patron of all time. Vergil and Horace were already in the circle. We have no external evidence for the relationship between Maecenas and Propertius, and the tone of this and III.9 (also addressed to him) is hard to judge. Maecenas is portrayed by those he sponsored as a genial, arty type, but there is no doubt he was also a loyal servant of Augustus, tasked with getting writers behind the emperor and promoting his message. From now on, Propertius is increasingly concerned with what kind of poetry he is going to write. In this and other pieces he says about as clearly as he can that Maecenas is pressing him to produce 'regime poetry'. Here, Propertius elegantly deflects the request, saying love poetry is all he is good for, and can be its own sort of epic or history. See my afterword for more on this theme.

Titans ... giants: Both waged unsuccessful wars against the gods, according to Greek mythology. The giants piled Mt Ossa on Mt Olympus, and Mt Pelion on Ossa (all mountains in Greece) in an attempt to reach heaven.

Xerxes: The (historical) Persian king who, in his second campaign against Greece in 480 BC, cut a canal through the Mt Athos peninsula.

Romulus: The legendary first king of Rome, supposedly suckled, along with his brother Remus, by a she-wolf.

Carthage: A power centre in what is now Tunisia, against which Rome fought the Punic Wars in the third and second centuries BC. Its biggest threat came when Hannibal invaded Italy.

Cimbri: A Germanic tribe who made an incursion into Italy in 102–101 BC but were defeated by the Roman general Marius. Ezra Pound's rendering of 'Cimbrorum minas' (the threats of the Cimbri) as 'Welsh mines' sparked ridicule from classical scholars.

Modena…: After Julius Caesar's assassination, Modena, north of Bologna, was the scene of an early clash between rival factions in 43 BC. The Battle of Philippi, where Octavian and Antony defeated Brutus and Cassius, came the following year. In 36 BC Sextus Pompeius, son of Caesar's rival Pompey the Great, was defeated in a naval battle off northern Sicily. The following line mentioning the 'ancient Etruscan race' raises again the fighting at Perugia mentioned in Book One. All these references are ambivalent since the battles concerned were still open wounds for many Romans, and we know from 1.22 (qv) that Propertius felt strongly about the Perugian slaughter. Slightly less controversial, perhaps, is what happened later. Octavian finished off the challenge from Antony and Cleopatra at the naval Battle of Actium in 31 BC. He went on to conquer Egypt, including the island of Pharos, off Alexandria, the site of a lighthouse that was one of the seven wonders of the ancient world. He staged a triumphal procession in Rome in 29 to mark his Egyptian victory, progressing along the Sacred Way through the Forum towards the Capitol. The Nile, symbol of Egypt, would have been portrayed in a model including the seven channels of its delta.

Callimachus: The acknowledged master of the third-century-BC Alexandrian school of Greek poetry, who lived from c. 305–c. 240.

Jupiter's showdown with the giant: Another reference to the war between the gods and giants. Propertius names the giant Enceladus, who was struck by Jupiter with a thunderbolt and confined under Mt Etna in Sicily.

Trojan forebears: Augustus was the adopted son of Julius Caesar, whose family traced its origins back to Aeneas of Troy, hero of Vergil's *Aeneid*.

Dulce et decorum est…: I was not able to resist conflating Propertius' *'laus in amore mori'* (there is glory in dying for love) with the *'dulce et decorum est pro patria mori'* (it is sweet and honourable to die for one's country) of Horace (and Wilfred Owen).

Phaedra…: The wife of Theseus who attempted to seduce her stepson Hippolytus, as related in Euripides' *Hippolytus* and (in an updated form) in Jules Dassin's 1962 film *Phèdre*, starring Melina Mercouri and Anthony Perkins. Circe, who detained Odysseus on his way home from the Trojan War, and Jason's lover Medea were described as witches, but the use of love potions by the three women is mentioned only by Propertius.

Philoctetes: A Greek fighter at Troy who suffered a poisoned leg, which was cured, according to Propertius, by the warrior-physician **Machaon,** mentioned in Homer. The Centaur **Chiron** restored sight to **Phoenix,** who had been blinded by his father. The 'doctor god' Aesculapius resurrected **Androgeon,** son of King Minos of Crete. **Telephus,** king of Mysia in Asia

Minor, was wounded by the spear of Achilles but healed by application of rust from the same weapon.

Tantalus: For disclosing the secrets of the gods, he was tempted forever in the underworld by fruit (or in other versions, water) that constantly withdrew from his grasp (hence the word 'tantalise'). The daughters of **Danaus**, who killed their husbands, were condemned to try to fill with water a jar that always leaked it out. The demi-god **Prometheus**, for giving the gift of fire to mortals, was punished by being chained to a rock in the Caucasus mountains, where every day a bird of prey tore out his entrails, which grew again overnight – as told in the play *Prometheus Bound*, attributed to Aeschylus.

British chariot: 'A fast two-wheeled vehicle used by Gauls and Britons as a war-chariot, but taken over by the Romans for pleasure and travel.' (Commentary by W. A. Camps).

II.2

In 'A Thought from Propertius', Yeats adapted part of this poem (apparently thinking of Maud Gonne): 'She might, so noble from head / To great shapely knees, / The long flowing line, / Have walked to the altar / Through the holy images / At Pallas Athene's side, / Or been fit spoil for a Centaur / Drunk with the unmixed wine.' (The couplet from which Yeats' last two lines are taken is considered by the Oxford and Loeb editors to have strayed in from some other poem and is not in my translation).

The Gorgon: The three Gorgons had snakes for hair and their glance turned men to stone. One, Medusa, was slain by the hero Perseus and her head was taken by the goddess Athene (Minerva to the Romans) to wear on her breastplate.

You goddesses: In the famous judgment of Paris, the goddesses Hera (Roman Juno), Aphrodite (Venus) and Athene stripped naked on Mount Ida, near Troy, for the shepherd Paris to decide which was the most beautiful. He chose Aphrodite, who rewarded him with the most beautiful woman in Greece, Helen, thus precipitating the Trojan War.

Sibyl of Cuma: A prophetess said to have lived for more than 700 years.

II.3

'You said ...: Medieval manuscripts were thin on punctuation, but modern editors agree that the first four lines of the poem represent an address to Propertius by an imaginary acquaintance, or perhaps by his *alter ego*. Hence my quotation marks.

Another book ... : This phrase is taken as confirmation that here we are near the beginning of Propertius' second volume of verse. While readers would surely have assumed that Cynthia was the woman hyperbolically praised in this poem, she is not actually identified here and her name does not appear until the fifth poem of the book. It is mentioned significantly less in the second book than in the first.

Ariadne: After being abandoned by Theseus (see note to 1.3) and rescued by Bacchus, Ariadne is portrayed by Propertius as leading the dances of Bacchus' maenad followers.

Sappho: The seventh-century-BC Greek lyric poet from the island of Lesbos. What little remains of her verse confirms her high reputation in antiquity.

Corinna: A sixth-century-BC poet from the Boeotia region of Greece.

Erinna: Another Greek woman poet, contemporary with Sappho and also from Lesbos. The name, however, is a conjecture for an obscure reading in the manuscripts.

Signalled a good omen: The Latin text literally says 'sneezed a good omen'. Sneezing was seen by the ancients as presaging good luck. **Jupiter** was known for his conquests among the beauties of Greek mythology, but not among the women of Roman legend.

Helen's beauty: Helen, wife of the Greek prince Menelaus, eloped with her lover Paris to Troy (also known as Pergamum). The Greek campaign to get her back became the Trojan War. In Christopher Marlowe's phrase, hers was 'the face that launched a thousand ships'. Achilles, the leading Greek warrior, was killed in the conflict. Priam was the king of Troy and the reference here is to a passage in Homer's *Iliad* in which he says it is not surprising that Greeks and Trojans should make war over a woman such as Helen.

II.4

The text of this poem is most uncertain. Heyworth prints it as a series of fragments (his lacunas represented by dots in my translation) and indicates he does not think it either begins or ends where the manuscripts have it. Since the theme is unified – falling in love with a woman spells trouble – the disjointed thought sequence will perhaps be less bothersome to today's general reader.

Perimede: Mentioned as a sorceress by the third-century-BC Greek poet Theocritus.

The pleasures of a boy: This and 1.20 (about Gallus' passion for a boy named Hylas) are Propertius' only significant references to pederasty, although bisexuality was taken for granted by many other Greek and Latin poets.

It is noteworthy that in both poems, love of boys – whatever its merits – is mentioned as something for other men. Propertius consistently portrays himself as, for better or worse (in this case, clearly for worse), an unreconstructed heterosexual.

II.5

Juno: The patron of marriage, and hence of relationships.

Cynthia so lovely ...: Reading the conjecture *'verna levis'* (literally 'a flighty slut') for the insult in the second half of the line. The manuscripts have *'verba levis'*, which would mean Cynthia's word was unreliable, but this seems too feeble to make her blanch for the rest of her life. At this distance, it is hard to judge exactly what tone Propertius was trying to convey, or how it would have been taken by his readers.

II.6

Lais ... Thais ... Phryne: Three celebrated courtesans in historical Greece. Lais, from Corinth, lived in the fifth century BC. Thais, born in Athens in the fourth century BC, accompanied Alexander the Great on his campaigns and is said to have instigated the burning of Persepolis. She was the subject of a Greek comedy by Menander (342–291 BC), a line from which is quoted in the New Testament at 1 Corinthians 15.33: 'Evil communications corrupt good manners.' She is not to be confused with the Thais (also a former courtesan) who lived in Egypt in the fourth century AD and was the subject of an 1890 novel by Anatole France and an 1894 opera by Jules Massenet. Phryne, famed as a great beauty despite her unflattering nickname ('toad' in Greek – her real name was Mnesarete), was born in Boeotia around 371 BC. Propertius alludes to the story that she became so rich that she offered to pay for the reconstruction of Thebes, which had been flattened by Alexander in 336. Her condition, apparently not accepted, was to put up an inscription: 'Destroyed by Alexander, restored by Phryne the courtesan.' Another sensational, if unverifiable, story is that she was tried for impiety but acquitted after her lawyer lowered her dress to bare her breasts before the judges. Phryne was said to be the model for the sculpture *Aphrodite of Knidos* by Praxiteles (one of her lovers). All three women inspired paintings by artists from the Renaissance onwards.

The Centaurs: In Greek mythology, Centaurs were invited to the wedding feast of Pirithous and Laodamia (not to be confused with the woman of the same name in 1.2, qv) of the Lapith tribe. They got drunk and attempted to rape the bride, leading to a battle.

Romulus: See note to II.1. The well-known story of the rape of the Sabine women (the primary meaning of the Latin *raptio* is in fact 'kidnapping') in 750 BC, three years after the foundation of Rome, relates how the Romans abducted women from the Sabine tribe, living to the north-east, to make good a shortage in their new city. The theme has been abundantly treated in painting.

Temples of Chastity: See note to 1.16.

Wives of Admetus and Ulysses: In mythology, respectively Alcestis, who gave her own life in place of her husband's after he offended the goddess Artemis (Diana), and Penelope, who waited ten years for her husband to return home after the Trojan War.

II.7

The law: While this poem may not be autobiographical, it does glance tantalisingly on the reality of love and marriage in ancient Rome, in contrast to what we read in literature. Propertius is apparently referring to the abrogation of a law promoting matrimony introduced in the Triumviral period in the 30s BC. Augustus was concerned by the low birth-rate among ethnic Romans and Italians compared with that of foreign immigrants. He returned to the issue after this poem was written, passing in 18 BC the Julian Law on Marriage, which sought to ban unions between different social classes and penalise bachelors and childless couples. Similar laws, with more stringent penalties, were introduced later, to great opposition.

Split us up: The narrator appears to say that the law would have compelled him to marry, thus ending his liaison with Cynthia. Critics have asked: why could 'Propertius' not have married 'Cynthia' herself? The answer, presumably, is that a well-born Roman man could not have married a woman of her profession.

Castor's great horse: A mighty steed, Castor being a famed horse-breaker. Propertius returns to the metaphor of love as a kind of warfare, one much worthier than the conventional kind. The poem is remarkable for its contemptuous references to Augustus' military goals, even allowing for the traditional nature of the *militia amoris* pose.

II.8

My friend: The friend is not named. Propertius goes on, later in the poem, to address first himself and then Cynthia.

Haemon ... Antigone: In the story made famous by Sophocles' play, Antigone, daughter of Oedipus, illegally buries her brother Polynices after he is killed in a bid to seize the throne of Thebes from another brother, Eteocles, who also dies. The new ruler, Creon, orders Antigone to be shut up in a vault, where she kills herself. When her fiancé Haemon, Creon's son, finds her body, he too commits suicide.

Achilles...: In the myth behind Homer's *Iliad*, Achilles, the principal Greek fighter at Troy, sulks in his tent and refuses to campaign after his slave and concubine, Briseis, is taken from him by the Greek commander, Agamemnon. As a result, the Trojans, led by Hector, threaten to overwhelm the Greeks. Hector kills Achilles' best friend, Patroclus. Briseis is finally returned, after which Achilles goes back to the front and kills Hector. Propertius' version differs slightly from Homer's, which has Achilles initially refusing Agamemnon's compensation but returning to the fray after Patroclus dies. Propertius also mentions Achilles' mother, the sea-goddess Thetis, and the armour specially made for him by the smith-god Hephaestus (Roman Vulcan).

II.9

Penelope: See also note to II.6. The Trojan War lasted ten years and Ulysses' wanderings around the Mediterranean another ten, as recounted in the *Odyssey*. Penelope successfully fended off suitors who argued Ulysses must be dead. One of her tricks was to say she must finish a funeral shroud for her ageing father-in-law, which she wove during the day and unpicked at night. The suitors took three years to tumble to the ruse.

Briseis: See note to II.8. Achilles was killed in the Trojan War by an arrow that pierced his vulnerable heel.

Simois: A river near Troy, thought to be now the Dumrek in north-western Turkey.

Styx's waters: The ancients believed the dead had to cross the River Styx to reach the underworld. Propertius is saying Cynthia nearly died, presumably of an illness. As usual, we need not see historical facts here, but there is a contrast with 1.15, where Propertius claims Cynthia was slow to show up when he was in grave, but unspecified, danger.

Libyan shoals: Sandbanks off the coast of Libya were a notorious hazard. Propertius mentions the Syrtes after which the modern Libyan town of Sirt is named.

The stars...: These two lines pick up a commonplace of ancient poetry, the lover waiting through the night outside the closed door of his beloved (see 1.16).

II.10

Heyworth and some other scholars believe lines have been lost before the start of the poem as transmitted by the manuscripts (where the Latin text begins with the word 'But'). In addition, some take the theme, with its teasing promise to move from erotic verse to epic at some future point, as confirmation that what we now have as Book Two was originally two books. If so, this poem would have been the last one in the first of those two volumes (or perhaps the first in the second). In any case, Propertius is returning to the issue he broached in ii.1 – pressure from the regime to switch subject matter. Here he goes a little further, saying he *will* do so – only to backtrack almost immediately and protest that he is not yet up to it. The poem's last word is 'Love'.

Helicon: A mountain in the Greek region of Boeotia, north of the Gulf of Corinth (modern Greek Elikonas). According to legend, two springs on it were sacred to the Muses, hence the mountain became a metaphor for poetry. It was also associated with the Greek poet Hesiod, who grew up in the small town of Ascra on its slopes. The principal surviving poems of Hesiod, who is thought to have lived in the eighth or seventh century BC, are the *Theogony*, on the origin of the universe, and the *Works and Days*, which praises labour, especially agriculture. Propertius, at the end of the present poem, signifies his inability to rise to epic by saying he has not yet climbed the heights of Helicon, but only got as far as a stream named Permessus, which flowed at its base.

The Leader: Augustus.

The Euphrates…: The Parthians were an Iranian people who, at their height, controlled swathes of the Middle East. The Romans fought them on and off for centuries, without ever subjugating them. In the Battle of Carrhae, near what is now Sanliurfa in south-eastern Turkey, in 53 BC, the famously wealthy Roman commander Marcus Licinius Crassus and his son were killed, and the army's standards captured, a major humiliation. Some 20,000 Roman soldiers died in one of the worst military defeats in Roman history. The Euphrates River, which rises in Turkey and flows through Syria into Iraq, passes to the west of the battlefield. Augustus prepared a major campaign against the Parthians, but eventually cut a deal with them, whereby the standards were returned in 20 BC. Propertius refers to a battle tactic often mentioned by Roman writers, in which the Parthians pretended to retreat, then fired arrows backward at their pursuers.

India: According to the late Roman historian Orosius, the Indians sent peace envoys to Augustus when he was on campaign in Tarragona, Spain, in 26 or 25 BC.

Arabia: The Roman commander Aelius Gallus led a campaign to Arabia in 25 BC, but his forces were decimated by its harsh climate. The 'country cowering at the world's end' may be Britain.

II.11

Most modern editors consider these enigmatic lines to be the close of a longer poem whose first part has been lost.

II.13

Arrows in Persia: Propertius may be thinking of the Parthians (see note to II.10). **Helicon:** See note to II.10. The mention of 'slender' Muses indicates love poetry rather than epic.
Linus: A son of Apollo who was a legendary musician. According to some versions of the myth, he was the teacher of Orpheus. Propertius touches on Orpheus' ability to charm animals and trees with his playing, but would like it to be Cynthia who is bewitched.
Persephone: Queen of the underworld. Her Latin name was Proserpina, but Propertius uses the Greek form. His reference to 'three slim volumes' has been taken by some as supporting the theory that what we have as Book Two of his poems was originally Books Two and Three.
Tomb of Achilles: The description of Achilles' tomb as 'bloody' apparently refers to a myth that, after the fall of Troy, Polyxena, daughter of the Trojan king Priam, was sacrificed over it at the demand of Achilles' ghost.
The sister Fates: The ancients believed that the three Fates, sisters whose Greek names were Clotho, Lachesis and Atropos, spun the thread of life.
Nestor: A Greek king, noted for his longevity, who accompanied the expedition to Troy, where his son Antilochus was killed in battle.
Adonis: As recounted in Shakespeare's poem, the beauty of Adonis caused Venus to fall in love with him. But he was killed by a boar while hunting on a mountain in Cyprus.

II.14

Electra ... Orestes: Daughter and son of Agamemnon, the Greek commander at Troy. In an episode used by Sophocles, Orestes came home in disguise, reporting his own death. Electra was initially deceived, then let in on the secret. **Ariadne**, daughter of King Minos of Crete, helped Theseus slay the Minotaur by giving him a ball of thread which he unwound as he made his way into the labyrinth where the monster was kept. After killing it he used the thread to get out. (See also note to I.3).

Victory over the Parthians: See note to II.10. This is not the only poem in which Propertius pokes fun at military 'triumphs' – parades in which victorious Roman generals showed off their spoils – and prefers his own amorous triumphs.

It's your decision…: Some scholars feel the last four lines are anticlimactic after the couplet Propertius proposes to write on Venus' temple, and are perhaps out of place. But it is typical of him to introduce a note of uncertainty at the end. Critics note that the four mythological examples that open the poem all have ambivalent sequels. Agamemnon was killed by his wife Clytemnestra when he got home. Orestes then killed Clytemnestra, but for that murder was hounded by the Furies. Ariadne was abandoned by Theseus on the island of Naxos. Even Ulysses was forced to resume his wanderings.

II.15

Paris: See notes to II.2 and II.3.

Endymion: A beautiful youth with whom the moon goddess Luna fell in love. He sleeps perpetually, either as a gift from Jupiter or because he was asleep when Luna first saw him.

Actium: See Note to II.1.

II.16a

The governor: In I.8a, Cynthia is denounced for proposing to travel to the Balkans (known at the time as Illyricum) with an unidentified man – a plan she is said in I.8b to have later abandoned. Those in search of historical facts from Propertius' poems have conjectured that the same man is referred to here. Propertius portrays himself as resentful about Cynthia's profession (see also note to I.8a), but his advice to her here is to soak the homecoming governor for all he has so he will then leave Rome again to top up his funds on another foreign assignment.

II.16b

Tyre: The still existing city on the Lebanese coast, also familiar from the Bible, along with Sidon, mentioned at the end of this poem. They were the two main centres of the region known to the Romans as Phoenicia, and were famed for producing a reddish-purple dye used in up-market clothes. While our scanty knowledge of Propertius' life means nothing can be ruled out, there is no evidence he actually went to the Middle East or elsewhere in Asia, whether to buy gifts for a girlfriend or for any other purpose.

The Leader: Augustus himself, imitating Romulus' thatched hut.

A slave: While many slaves were treated badly, some made their fortunes and purchased their freedom. That did not protect them from the snobbery of well-born Romans. Propertius here laments that an ex-slave is now rich enough to buy Cynthia's services.

The leader who filled Actium Bay: This time the reference is to Mark Antony and the Battle of Actium. Cleopatra is reported to have pulled her Egyptian vessels out of the battle to head home, at which point Antony also turned tail and followed her.

Eriphyla: In Greek mythology, she took a bribe of a necklace to induce her husband Amphiaraus to join the campaign of the 'Seven Against Thebes' (see note to I.7). He died in the conflict, and Eriphyla was killed by one of their sons in retribution.

Creusa: A Corinthian princess for whom Jason, the Argonauts' leader, abandoned Medea, who sent Creusa a present of a crown, which set her on fire.

Jupiter: The gods often took a lenient view of infidelity, but Propertius says this is not always so. While mortals such as Ixion were punished for falling in love with Jupiter's wife, Juno, there are no stories of him being betrayed by her, whereas his own philandering was notorious.

Pleiades, Orion: 'The setting of these constellations in October–November marked a stormy season.' (Camps).

II.17

Tantalus ... Sisyphus: Examples frequently cited by Propertius of punishments in the underworld for misdeeds on earth. On Tantalus, see note to II.1. Sisyphus had to roll a rock uphill, only for it always to topple down again when he was near the summit.

II.18

The thirty-eight lines found here in the manuscripts are among the most chaotic in the Propertian corpus. Scholars believe they come from two or even three original poems, none of them apparently complete. I have followed the Oxford Text in ending at 'before long', forming a substantial chunk of a poem that contrasts Cynthia's behaviour with the devotion of the Dawn goddess to her ageing husband. Even so, it is not easy to see what connects the first four lines to the rest. I have not translated eighteen lines, printed by Heyworth as fragments, which in part condemn the use of make-up and hair-dye (in the manner of I.2) and which clearly belong to a different poem.

Tithonus: The Dawn goddess (Aurora in Latin) fell in love with the mortal Tithonus, son of the Trojan hero Laomedon. He (or she) asked the gods for his immortality, which was granted, but forgot to ask for perpetual youth, so he grew older and older. Ancient poetry portrays Dawn as boarding her chariot in the east every morning to bring light to the world. A recently discovered fragment of Sappho describes her as embracing Tithonus in his youth.

Memnon: The son of Dawn, he was killed by Achilles at Troy.

II.19

Deserting Rome: Propertius does not say why Cynthia is going to the country. We are doubtless dealing again with an imaginary scenario.

Diana: The goddess of hunting.

Clitunno: This small river (Clitumnus in Latin) rises from the rock in a series of springs a few miles north of Spoleto in Umbria. Its beauty, and its reputation for making cattle that bathed in it sparkling white, were hymned by poets from Vergil to Goethe, Byron and Carducci, but would have had a special resonance for Propertius, who was born nearby. The springs, forming a pool surrounded by poplars, are still a tourist attraction.

II.20

Briseis ... Andromache: On Briseis, see note to II.8. Andromache, wife of the Trojan hero Hector (killed by Achilles), was among the widows of Troy who, after the sack of the city, fell into the hands of the Greek army.

Mourning dove: A compression and adaptation of the Latin. Propertius mentions the nightingale, whose song was portrayed by ancient writers as a lament, in reference to the myth of Procne (on whom see more extensive note to III.10).

Niobe: She boasted of having more children than the goddess Latona, who had two – the gods Apollo and Diana. As a punishment, all Niobe's twelve children were killed and she was turned into an ever-weeping rock on Mt Sipylus (now Mt Spil in western Turkey, where a rock resembling a human face can still be seen). 'Like Niobe, all tears,' says Shakespeare in *Hamlet*.

Danae: Her father Acrisius, king of Argos in Greece, locked her up in an iron (or bronze) chamber after a prophecy that any son of hers would kill him. Zeus (Jupiter), who lusted after Danae, managed to visit her in the chamber in the form of a shower of gold. The result was the hero Perseus, who did eventually kill Acrisius by accident.

Furies of tragedy: The Greek tragedians Aeschylus and Euripides wrote of

Orestes being pursued by the Furies after he killed his mother, Clytemnestra, for murdering his father, Agamemnon.

Aeacus: One of the judges of the underworld.

Tityus ... Sisyphus: Tityus, a giant, was condemned to have vultures everlastingly feed on his entrails for an attempted sexual assault on Latona. On Sisyphus, whose offence was to reveal divine secrets, see note to II.17.

II.21

Panthus: As in several other poems, a Greek pseudonym is used to denote a Roman acquaintance. Unless we again have an entirely imaginary scenario, there is background to this poem that we don't know, although evidently Panthus is the 'pretty-boy lover' referred to a few lines further on. 'Panthus has been writing verse slanders about Propertius ... and this has helped him become a lover of Cynthia. One assumes that her name too has featured in his poetry.' (Heyworth).

Dodona: See note to I.9.

His Colchian hostess: Medea. On her, Jason and Creusa, see note to II.16b.

Calypso: See note to I.15. The *Odyssey* does not say Ulysses 'gave her the slip' but that she facilitated his departure, despite not wanting him to go.

II.22a

Demophoon: As with Panthus in II.21, the Greek name is intended to disguise some Roman friend of Propertius. He does not appear in any other work by the poet, although II.24b (qv) refers to the mythological Demophoon.

The theatre: We know from Propertius and other writers that theatres, like street-corners, were pick-up places, or at least locations where prostitutes plied their trade. Some did this in the audience but in ancient Rome, as in some other cultures, certain actresses, singers and dancers were considered fair game by men.

Phrygian tune: Propertius is referring to ecstatic cults that involved self-harm during dances. Phrygia, in what is now Turkey, was often cited as a hotbed of these religions.

Thamyras: A mythical Thracian *chansonnier* who challenged the Muses to a song contest. If he won, he could have sex with them all in turn. If not, they could deprive him of whatever they liked. Predictably, the Muses won and took away Thamyras' sight and singing abilities. Propertius says ironically that even if he too lost his sight (and by implication his poetic gift) he would still pursue attractive women.

II.22b

Jupiter: The king of the gods assumed the likeness of the warrior Amphitryon, while he was away on campaign, in order to bed his wife Alcmena. To enhance the night of passion, he doubled its length by delaying the rotation of the stars.

Briseis: See note to II.8. On **Andromache**, see note to II.20.

II.23–24a

Propertius' argument that it is less damaging to his reputation to consort with common prostitutes than to be messed around by a higher-class woman such as Cynthia or chase after married women is a theme that crops up elsewhere in Latin literature. The stern moralist Cato is said to have advised young men to sow their wild oats by visiting brothels.

Sacred Way: Whether or not Propertius is making ironic play with the name, the Sacred Way (Via Sacra in Latin), one of ancient Rome's main streets, is presented here as a place to find both street-walkers and gift shops.

Orontes and Euphrates: In ancient times, as in modern, many of the prostitutes on the streets of the developed world seem to have been immigrant women from less advanced regions, in this case pre-Islamic Syria.

'How can you say that...?': The questioner is evidently an imaginary interlocutor, friend or reader.

II.24b

Many scholars believe that between '...Amor changes direction?' and 'Let this man compete...' the manuscript tradition has lost some lines that would introduce the rival for the affections of Cynthia (if it is she) who is discussed in the second part of the poem.

Hydra of Lerna ... Hesperides: Killing the Hydra, a water-serpent at Lerna in the Greek Peloponnese, and taking apples from the garden of the Hesperides sisters, protected by a snake in the far west of the then known world, were two of the twelve labours of Hercules. The labours, which Hercules carried out as a penance, are specifically mentioned a few lines further on.

Theseus' love...: On Theseus and Ariadne, see note to I.3. **Demophoon**, son of Theseus, had an affair with Phyllis, a Thracian princess, on his way back from the Trojan War, but then left her (she eventually committed suicide). On **Medea** and **Jason**, see note on Creusa in II.16b. Medea had helped Jason carry out a task set him by her father Aeetes in her homeland of Colchis (see also note on III.11).

II.25

Calvus ... Catullus: This is one of two passages (the other is in II.34) to name Catullus (c. 84–c. 54 BC), whom Propertius must have seen as an important predecessor. Calvus (82–c. 47 BC) was a friend of Catullus and mentioned in his poems. Both were members of a group of 'new poets' that the conservative Cicero made fun of. Only a few fragments survive of Calvus' poetry and of his oratory, for which he was also noted.

Tithonus or Nestor: On Tithonus, see note to II.18. On Nestor, see note to II.13. Both are cited here because of the advanced age to which they lived.

Cruel Perillus' bull: Perillus was an artisan who was said to have constructed for Phalaris, the sixth-century-BC tyrant of Agrigento in Sicily, a bronze bull in which his victims could be roasted, their cries making the bull appear to roar. Perillus himself became the first victim of the contraption.

Caucasus vultures: A reference to Prometheus, on whom see note to II.1.

You, my friend ... : As often, Propertius changes addressee – in this case, from Cynthia to an unnamed friend. Some have speculated that the man concerned was another competitor for Cynthia's affections, but the tone seems too equable for that. Before the poem ends, Propertius again switches audience, to men who want a variety of girlfriends. The argument made is the exact opposite of that a few poems earlier, in II.22b.

II.26a

This poem was imitated by André Chénier in 'Chrysé', one of his *Idylles marines*.

Ionian Sea: Off the west coast of Greece.

Helle: In Greek mythology, a Theban princess who, persecuted by her stepmother Ino, fled with her brother on the back of a magic gold-fleeced ram. She fell off and drowned in the strait that was named the Hellespont after her (now the Dardanelles in Turkey). Ino, attacked by her husband, leapt into the sea to escape him and was turned into a sea-goddess named Leucothoe.

Castor, Pollux: See note to I.17.

Glaucus: A sea-god who started life as a fisherman, but became immortal after eating a magic herb.

Nesaee, Cymothoe: Sea-nymphs mentioned by Homer.

Arion: A musician said to have thrown himself off a ship into the sea to escape sailors who were trying to rob him, and to have been rescued by a dolphin.

II.26b

Ulysses: 'Alluding to the wrecking of the Greek armada on the return from Troy by Nauplius, who lit beacons to lure them on the rocks of Caphareus (a promontory of Euboea) in revenge for the death of his son Palamedes, whose conviction for treachery Ulysses had procured by means of manufactured evidence.' (Camps). Others take it as referring to the contrary winds that held up the departure of the Greek fleet for Troy from the island of Euboea (Evia) off the east coast of Greece.

Two rocks: The Symplegades, or clashing rocks – in mythology, two moving islands at the north end of the Bosphorus, which butted together when anything tried to pass between them. But the Argo made it after a dove had been sent to fly through first.

Amymone: Daughter of Danaus, legendary founder of the city of Argos, she was sent out in search of water at Lerna in the Peloponnese. She was rescued from the advances of a satyr by Neptune, who, however, proceeded to enjoy her himself. To reward her, he then struck the ground with his trident, causing a spring to gush forth and enabling her to take water home.

Orithyia: An Athenian princess carried off by Boreas, the god of the north wind. Two sons resulted, Calais and Zetes, mentioned in 1.20.

Scylla ... Charybdis: The names have passed into proverb, but in mythology, Scylla was imagined as a female sea-monster living in a cave opposite Charybdis, a whirlpool across the Straits of Messina. Together they constituted a mortal hazard to shipping.

Auriga: I have used the name by which this constellation is known to modern astronomers. Propertius speaks of Haedus (The Kid), one of the stars in the constellation. The rising of Orion and Auriga in the autumn was associated with stormy weather.

To lay down my life ...: Propertius is apparently returning to the thought expressed earlier in the poem, that he would be content to be lost at sea if Cynthia was granted decent burial on land.

II.28

The oldest Propertius manuscript, followed by some modern editors, makes this two poems, the second beginning at 'The magician's wand...'. But the theme – Cynthia close to death – seems to persist throughout. If, at the end, the story has moved on and Cynthia has been saved, the effect is similar to that of a medieval or Renaissance painting in which successive episodes appear on the same canvas. As in many other poems, Propertius has created a dramatic scenario and we need see no reference to actual events. Ezra Pound was so struck by this poem that he made two English versions of it: 'Prayer for his Lady's Life' (1911), which translates a section near the end in the archaising style of his earlier period; and a rendering of the full text in Sections VIII and IX of *Homage to Sextus Propertius* (written in 1917), in a more modern idiom.

Venus ... Juno ... Minerva: By chance or design, the three goddesses who competed in the judgment of Paris, which led to the Trojan War. On Juno, see note to II.5. Minerva (Greek Athene) is habitually described in Homer as 'grey-eyed'. There are hints in ancient literature that the colour was thought unbecoming.

Io: See also note to 1.3. After being driven round the world by a gadfly sent by Juno, she was changed back from a cow to her proper form in Egypt, where she became identified with the Egyptian goddess Isis. She is referred to again in the penultimate line.

Ino: See note to II.26a.

Callisto: An Arcadian woman beloved by Jupiter. She was turned into a bear – either by him or by Juno – and was killed by the hunting goddess Diana. Jupiter then transformed her into the Great Bear constellation.

Semele: Yet another of Jupiter's women and the subject of a well-known opera by Handel. The jealous Juno incited her to persuade the king of the gods to appear to her in his full resplendence, as a result of which Semele was burnt to a cinder.

Persephone: See note to II.13. Her husband Pluto was king of the underworld.

Europa ... Pasiphae ... Antiope ... Tyro: Europa was a Phoenician princess carried off by Jupiter disguised as a bull. Pasiphae, wife of King Minos of Crete, was smitten with desire for (another) bull. In order to couple with it, she had the craftsman Daedalus construct a hollow wooden cow, which she lay inside. The result was the Minotaur, half-man, half-bull. See notes to 1.4 on Antiope and 1.13 on Tyro.

Achaia: A part of ancient Greece.

II.29b

Vesta: Goddess of the household, and famously chaste. The ancients believed that telling a deity of your ominous dreams could avert bad consequences.

II.30

This odd, disjointed poem or poems (lines may well be missing), starts with what appears to be advice to a friend about to travel abroad (possibly on the Parthian expedition mentioned in II.10), warning him that wherever he goes, he won't escape love. Then the addressee becomes Cynthia, with Propertius again defending his dedication to love (or love poetry) and protesting that only she can inspire him.

Pegasus: In mythology, the winged horse who sprang from Gorgon's blood and was ridden by the hero Bellerophon to slay the fire-breathing Chimaera monster.

Perseus: The slayer of the Gorgon was helped by winged sandals given him by the gods. Such sandals were associated with the messenger god Mercury. Propertius describes the air as 'Mercury's high road'.

Old buffers: Probably another echo of Catullus' Poem 5: 'Lesbia, live with me / & love me so / we'll laugh at all / the sour-faced strict- / ures of the wise.' (Whigham's translation).

Maeander: Identified as the modern Büyük Menderes River in south-western Turkey. The ancient name is the origin of the word 'meander'. Propertius is referring to a legend that the goddess Minerva invented the flute but threw it away after seeing a reflection of herself with her cheeks puffed out playing it, and finding it unflattering.

Semele ... Io ...: On Semele, see note to II.28, and on Io, notes to I.3 and II.28. In an ironic reversal, Propertius makes it Jupiter who is burned rather than Semele, and Jupiter who is undone rather than Io. He goes on to cite another myth that the bisexual king of the gods assumed the form of an eagle to carry off the beautiful Trojan prince Ganymede, a subject treated by numerous artists over the ages.

Oeagrus: In legend, a Thracian king who begot the singer Orpheus in a liaison with the Muse Calliope.

When they put you ...: Bacchus, as well as Apollo, had the power of poetic inspiration. But Propertius is saying that 'only when Cynthia accompanies him to the Muses' haunts will inspiration come to him; he cannot receive it from the Muses alone.' (Camps).

II.31–32

Apollo's gilded portico: Vowed by Octavian (Augustus) after his victory over Sextus Pompeius in 36 BC, it was dedicated by the emperor in 28. The complex included a temple, and Propertius appears to refer to two separate statues of Apollo, both portraying him singing. Ancient writers say that between the columns of the portico were statues of the fifty daughters of the mythical King Danaus, all but one of whom, Hypermnestra, carried out his orders to kill their bridegrooms on their collective wedding night.

Myron: A fifth-century-BC Greek sculptor.

Delos: The Aegean island was the reputed birthplace of Apollo.

The Gauls: Invading Gauls attacked Delphi, Greece, but were defeated there in 278 BC. Mount Parnassus overlooks the city.

Niobe: See note to II.20.

Diana's grove: At Ariccia, south of Rome. Propertius goes on to list other towns near the capital: Palestrina (later the birthplace of the sixteenth-century Italian composer of that name, but known to the ancient Romans as Praeneste), Tuscolo (now ruined), Tivoli (ancient Tibur) and Lanuvio. The Appian Way, one of the great Roman roads, went ultimately to Brindisi, south-eastern Italy. The poet's point is that Cynthia is visiting these places not for lack of attractions in Rome but to escape his surveillance and dally with other men. Lanuvio figures at greater length in IV.8, which has echoes of this poem.

Pompey's portico: Different from Apollo's portico and mentioned in IV.8 as a pick-up place.

Maro: It is uncertain who this is, but a man of the name is mentioned by Homer as a priest of Apollo and by Euripides as a son of Bacchus. Camps suggests he may have been depicted in a statue as a satyr, with fountain-water spilling from his mouth. **Triton** was an attendant of Neptune and he too may have been carved in stone sporadically spouting water from a horn in the shape of a seashell.

Helen: Although her elopement with Paris sparked the ten-year-long Trojan War, when it ended after enormous casualties on both sides, she returned to live quietly in Sparta with her Greek husband Menelaus.

Venus: Married to the smith-god Vulcan, she had an affair with the war-god Mars.

A goddess: Some have seen this as a continuing reference to Venus, whose liaison with the Trojan Anchises led to the birth of Aeneas. But most modern commentators think it is the nymph Oenone, who had an *amour* with Paris on Mount Ida, near Troy.

Silenus: Chief of the satyrs, wood spirits conventionally depicted as half-man, half-goat and noted for their voracious sexual appetites.

Lesbia: An intriguing reference to the woman who was the subject of Catullus' love poems and who is widely thought to have been the historical figure Clodia (see Afterword). The words 'Rome is fortunate,' found just above, may echo a notorious bad line in a self-congratulatory poem by Cicero (who famously pilloried Clodia in a legal speech): '*O fortunatam natam me consule Romam*' (O fortunate Rome, born by my consulship). Propertius' poem combines (possibly ironic) praise of stern old-fashioned morality – which was preached by the likes of Cicero and was a rhetorical commonplace – with recognition that such an era, if it ever existed, was long over. Hence the poem's last line.

Saturn's reign: Sometimes named as an ancient king of Latium (Lazio, the area around Rome), Saturn was also identified as a Roman equivalent of the Greek Kronos, who was supplanted as king of the gods by his son Zeus (Jupiter). Saturn's rule is conventionally described by Latin writers as a golden age in the remote past.

The Flood: Classical mythology recorded a Great Flood resembling that in Genesis, with Deucalion as the equivalent of Noah.

King Minos' wife: Pasiphae, on whom see note to II.28.

Danae: See note to II.20.

II.33a

The 'plot' of the poem concerns the Egyptian goddess Isis, identified in classical mythology with Io (see notes to I.3 and II.28). The second stanza refers to her various manifestations. The cult of Isis reached Rome, attracting numerous women, who were required to forgo sex for ten days as part of an annual festival. Roman imperial authorities made at least two attempts to ban the cult during the 20s BC, but it returned.

II.33b

Ruin of good water: The ancients habitually mixed wine with water before drinking.

Icarius (or Icarus): Not to be confused with the Icarus who crashed into the sea while attempting to fly from Crete, he was, in mythology, an Athenian who was taught how to make wine by Bacchus. He gave a taste to some shepherds, who, when they became drunk, thought they had been poisoned and killed him. **Eurytion** was the Centaur who drunkenly attempted to molest the bride at the wedding of Pirithous the Lapith and Hippodamia (see note to II.6). The Cyclops Polyphemus, in Homer's *Odyssey*, allowed Ulysses and his crew to escape when they blinded him after intoxicating him with Ismarian wine, renowned as a strong brew.

Falernian: A famous ancient Roman wine from Campania, the area around Naples.

II.34

The bulk of the poem picks up the argument of I.9 (addressed to Ponticus) concerning an epic poet's need to shift to love poetry as a result of personal infatuation. But it also links to II.1 to develop Propertius' discussion of the incompatibility of the two kinds of poetry, effectively 'topping and tailing' Book Two – assuming the book was originally conceived in the form we now have it.

Menelaus' guest: The Trojan Paris (see note to II.3).

A man she barely knew: Jason.

Lynceus: A name that occurs nowhere else in Propertius. It is widely considered a pseudonym for Lucius Varius Rufus, a writer of epic and tragedy who introduced Horace to Maecenas and was later an editor of the *Aeneid* after Vergil's death. Only fragments of his work survive.

Epimenides: A semi-mythical poet and religious teacher from Crete, said to have lived in the sixth century BC. But this is based on the reading of only part of the manuscript tradition, and many other suggestions have been made. Whoever it is, Propertius' point is that his work can no longer help Lynceus because it is not about love.

Philitas ... Callimachus: On Callimachus, see note to II.1. Philitas, born on the eastern Mediterranean island of Kos, was another member of the Alexandrian school. He was slightly older than Callimachus, but his exact dates are unclear. Both are cited again as masters in the first poem of Book Three (qv).

Achelous: The largest river in Greece, flowing into the Ionian Sea. The line perhaps alludes to a mythical 'fight between Hercules and the (personified) Achelous over Deianira, in which the victor Hercules broke off one of his rival's horns (regular attributes of a river-god)' (Camps). Deianira later became Hercules' wife.

Maeander: See note to II.30.

Adrastus ... Archemorus: In mythology, Adrastus, king of the Greek city of Argos, went on the disastrous expedition of the Seven Against Thebes (see note to I.7). Hercules gave him the magic horse Arion, which had the gift of speech and saved Adrastus by predicting the defeat of the expedition. Earlier, Arion had won a victory at the first Nemean Games near Corinth (a regular fixture in historical times), which were held to mark the funeral of a child named Archemorus, killed by a snake.

Amphiaraus ... Capaneus: Other members of the Seven Against Thebes. Amphiaraus' chariot fell into a gap in the earth.

Antimachus and Homer: Antimachus was a Greek epic poet of the fifth century BC. He had a mistress named Lyde, while there was a story that Homer fell in love with Penelope.

Vergil: In this passage, picked up in Ezra Pound's *Homage* (Section XII),

Propertius looks ahead to the *Aeneid*, evidently aware that Vergil was working on it and of details in the text too. He goes on to mention Vergil's two other well-known works: the *Georgics*, a didactic poem on farming inspired by the *Works and Days* of 'old Hesiod'; and the *Eclogues*, which set the pastoral life described by the third-century-BC Greek poet Theocritus against the background of contemporary Italy. The following lines have a number of verbal echoes from the latter work, including the use of the word 'happy'.

Thyrsis and Daphnis: Shepherds' names from the *Eclogues*.

Galaesus: A river in southern Italy, which cannot be exactly identified.

Tityrus: Another of Vergil's shepherds. Because his name kicks off the first Eclogue, it was sometimes used as shorthand for the work as a whole and even as a pseudonym for Vergil. **Corydon** and **Alexis** feature in the second Eclogue.

Varro: A first-century-BC Latin poet who addressed love poems to a woman he called Leucadia.

Calvus: See note to II.25. He wrote an elegy on the death of his wife or mistress Quintilia.

Gallus: See note to I.5. Lycoris, the beloved in his almost entirely lost poems, is believed to have been a mime actress named Volumnia or Cytheris. Propertius and his readers would have known that Gallus did not die of love for Lycoris but committed suicide after incurring Augustus' displeasure. The reference to him here is an elegant farewell to a literary model, and possible early patron, of Propertius.

III.1

Callimachus, Philitas: See notes to II.1 and II.34.

Triumph: A parody of Rome's triumphal military processions, on which see note to II.14.

Sisters... daughters of Pegasus: The Muses.

Rivers of Troy: The rivers Scamander and Simois near Troy are portrayed by Homer as fighting with the Greek hero Achilles, who was later to kill the Trojan champion Hector and drag the body round the tomb of his friend Patroclus, slain by Hector (see also note to II.8). Hercules is described as capturing Troy twice, once on his own account in revenge because he was not given the reward promised him by King Laomedon for killing a monster, and the second time indirectly when his arrows were used by the Greek warrior Philoctetes to kill Paris.

III.2

Propertius' words at times resemble the better known lines of Horace, written around the same time in *Odes* III.30, beginning: *'Exegi monumentum aere perennius'* (I have wrought a monument more lasting than bronze).

Cithaeron: A mountain range near Thebes. On Amphion, see note to I.9.

Galatea: A sea-nymph beloved by Polyphemus, the one-eyed Cyclops living on the slopes of Mt Etna in Sicily. His wooing is sometimes portrayed by classical authors as uncouth and ridiculous, but is presented by Propertius as successful.

Gardens of Babylon: Propertius in fact refers to the legendary garden of King Alcinous, mentioned in Homer's *Odyssey*. The 'private water supply' is an allusion to the *aqua Marcia*, an aqueduct built in the second century BC by Quintus Marcius Rex to bring water to Rome from the Sabine hills to the east. Only rich people could have afforded their own water supply, piped off from the public aqueduct.

Jove's Olympia temple: The spectacular temple in southern Greece, built in the mid-fifth century BC, was one of the seven wonders of the ancient world, as were the Egyptian pyramids and the Mausoleum.

Original Mausoleum: Built of white marble at Halicarnassus, Asia Minor, for Mausolus, ruler of Caria, by his widow Artemisia in the mid-fourth century BC.

III.3

Helicon: See note to II.10. The 'stream struck by Pegasus' is Hippocrene (Greek for 'Horse Stream'), a nearby fountain sacred to the Muses, said to have been produced by a hoof-stroke of Pegasus (on which, see note to II.30).

Kings of Alba: A town south of Rome which Aeneas' son Ascanius built and where his descendants ruled until Romulus founded Rome.

Old Ennius: The first great Roman poet (239–169 BC), he wrote the *Annals* in eighteen books on Roman history, of which about 550 lines survive. There follows a jumbled account of some of the events he included (or not). The **Curiatii** and the **Horatii** fought each other on behalf of Rome and Alba, though it is uncertain who was on which side. The mention of **Aemilius** apparently refers to Aemilius Paullus, who was victorious over Perseus, king of Macedon, and celebrated a triumph in Rome in 167 BC, shipping huge quantities of booty up the Tiber. Since this was two years after Ennius died, he can hardly have written of it, but it would be unlike Propertius to scruple over such details. Quintus **Fabius** Maximus was given the title *Cunctator*

(Delayer) because his tactic of putting off an engagement with Hannibal weakened the Carthaginians and gave Rome time to recover in the Second Punic War. The Battle of **Cannae** in south-eastern Italy in 216 BC was a disastrous defeat by Hannibal in which up to 70,000 Roman soldiers died. The reference to the **guardian deities** (Latin Lares) is not entirely clear. The sacred **geese** featured in a celebrated episode in which their 'cackling … woke [the Roman consul Marcus] Manlius and saved the temple of Jupiter on the Capitol from being captured by the Gauls in 390 or 387' BC (Heyworth & Morwood's commentary).

Castalian copse: The geography is as muddled as the history. The Castalian spring, seen as a source of poetic inspiration, was on Mt Parnassus near Delphi, nowhere near Mt Helicon where the action of this poem starts.

Silenus: See note to II.31–32.

The Gorgon's pool: We are back to Hippocrene. Pegasus, its creator, sprang from the blood of the Gorgon Medusa's severed head.

The nine Wenches: The Muses.

Bacchic staffs: Known as *thyrsi*, they were 'fennel rods tipped with pine cones carried by the followers of Bacchus, god of wine, but also of drama' (Heyworth & Morwood).

Swan-drawn carriage: The swan has been a symbol of the poet until at least as recently as Mallarmé; it was also not infrequently said by poets to draw Venus' chariot, and thus served as a symbol of love.

Marius: See note to II.1 for his victories over German tribes.

Philitas: See note to II.34.

III.4

Divine Caesar: Augustus. He had been known as the son of a god since his adoptive father, Julius Caesar, was deified in 44 BC. Augustus himself received divine honours in the eastern empire after the Battle of Actium. On the projected Parthian campaign, see note to II.10. This poem evidently was written before the diplomatic solution was implemented in 20 BC.

Vesta: The fire in this goddess' temple in Rome was tended by the famous Vestal Virgins, who were required to keep it perpetually burning – otherwise the gods might be thought to have withdrawn their favour. See also note to II.29b.

Your descendant: Julius Caesar's family claimed descent from Aeneas, the refugee from Troy and legendary ancestor of the Romans. His arrival in Italy is recounted in Vergil's *Aeneid*. In Greek mythology, Aeneas was the son of Aphrodite (Venus).

III.5

Bronzes smelted in the sack of Corinth: The Romans captured the Greek city of Corinth in 144 BC. According to one story, fires caused the melting together of quantities of gold, silver and bronze, creating 'an alloy of enormous value' (Heyworth & Morwood).

Prometheus: Credited with having created the human race. See also note to II.1.

Acheron: A river of the underworld.

Jugurtha...Marius: Apart from his victories over the Germans (see note to II.1), the Roman commander Marius, after a seven-year struggle, also defeated Jugurtha, king of Numidia in North Africa, in 105 BC. Jugurtha was paraded in Marius' triumphal procession in Rome, then killed, as was the normal fate of captured enemy leaders.

Croesus...Irus: Croesus, sixth-century-BC king of Lydia in Asia Minor, was fabled for his wealth. Irus was a (mythological) beggar in Ithaca mentioned in Homer's *Odyssey*. He abused the returning Odysseus (Ulysses), who responded by beating him up.

Mount Pindus: In Greece. It is not known whether Propertius had a particular earthquake in mind.

Ploughman: Propertius is alluding to the constellation known as the Plough or Great Bear. It is described as slow because it is visible for ten months of the year in the Northern Hemisphere.

Pleiades: Also a constellation. According to Greek myth, the seven daughters of Atlas and Pleione.

Wheels and rocks, and thirst: A reference to the respective punishments of Ixion, Sisyphus and Tantalus in the underworld.

Alcmaeon...: Pursued by the Furies for killing his mother. **Phineus** was 'punished (for revealing too much in his prophecies) by the bird-like Harpies, who foul his food every time he tries to eat' (Heyworth & Morwood). **Tisiphone** was one of the Furies, portrayed as having snakes for hair.

Cerberus: The many-headed dog said to guard the underworld. On **Tityus**, see note to II.20.

Some fiction: As argued by Lucretius in his poem *De rerum natura* (On the Nature of the Universe), which expounds the ideas of the Greek philosopher Epicurus.

Standards of Crassus: See note to II.10.

III.6

No interpretation completely ties up all loose ends in the poem, but I have accepted the Oxford Text presentation, in the absence of quotation marks in the manuscripts. This implies: a) that there are three speakers – Propertius (who opens and closes the poem), Lygdamus, and Cynthia, whose statement is included in Lygdamus' report; b) that there is something missing in the text at the start of Lygdamus' speech, which otherwise begins too abruptly (and in the Latin ungrammatically); and c) that Lygdamus is – as in iv.8 and apparently iv.7 – the slave of Propertius, not of Cynthia. There is, however, a probable play on the double meaning of the Latin word '*domina*' (the same as that in its English translation, 'mistress'). Since Propertius is, in his turn, the 'slave' of Cynthia, Lygdamus is in a sense the servant of two masters – or a master and a mistress. This may explain why Propertius says at the end that Lygdamus could win his freedom 'if it's down to me' – implying that Cynthia may also have a say, and might not agree. At all events, the conniving slave is a staple of ancient comedy.

Herbs: The ancients believed that herbal brews could induce – or banish – love. Cynthia goes on to list magic devices and ingredients worthy of the witches in *Macbeth*.

III.7

Paetus: The poem, of the type known by the Greek word *epikedeion*, is one of the few in the Propertian collection that can truly be described as an elegy in the modern sense, being a lament for a certain Paetus, lost at sea. We have no independent information on him, although men of that name crop up sporadically at other periods of Roman history. It has been suggested that he may have been a relative of the poet. Scholars have not questioned the basic facts in the poem, indicating that the dead man was a young merchant whose ship capsized in a storm on the way to Alexandria, Egypt, possibly dragged by gales off its moorings at some Aegean harbour *en route*. The perils of seafaring were a commonplace of ancient poetry.

Kafireas' reefs: Referring to the wreck of the Greek fleet returning from Troy, on which see note to ii.26b.

Nereus: A marine deity. One of his sea-nymph daughters was **Thetis**, mother of Achilles.

North Wind: Anthropomorphised by the ancients variously as Boreas and Aquilo. On his abduction of Orithyia, see note to ii.26b.

III.9

Maecenas: The poem revisits the themes of II.1 (qv) and is again addressed to Maecenas, whom Propertius calls his *'fautor'*, meaning something like promoter. In this further *'recusatio'*, the poet argues that he is in effect copying Maecenas, who despite boasting Etruscan royal descent preferred to shun the limelight and did not hold top public offices. This, of course, did not diminish his power. When Octavian was away from Rome in 31–29 BC, he left Maecenas in charge of the city. Propertius notes that Maecenas was an *'eques'* – literally a knight but with different connotations from the English term and signifying the second tier in the Roman status pecking order (after senatorial rank).

Lysippus...: Propertius cites four pairs of famous Greek artists, stressing how their styles differed, just as his style differs from that of the epic writer. Lysippus was a fourth-century-BC sculptor from Sicyon in the northern Peloponnese, working in bronze. **Calamis** dated from the fifth century BC; none of his work survives. On **Apelles**, see note to I.2. **Parrhasius** came from Ephesus and his work was characterised by a fine attention to detail. **Mentor** (fourth century BC) and **Mys** (fifth century BC) were both silversmiths. **Phidias'** fifth-century-BC gold and ivory statue of Jupiter at Olympia (the temple there is mentioned in III.2) was renowned, but has not survived. **Praxiteles**, from the fourth century BC, was also an Athenian and worked sometimes in local marble.

Camillus: The famed Roman military leader was a private citizen in exile when he was called back to service to save Rome from the invasion of the Gauls in 387 BC.

Thebes: See note to I.7 on the failed attack by the 'Seven Against Thebes'. The sons of the Seven, however, later returned and sacked Thebes.

Ploughed over: In ancient times, ploughing over the walls of a defeated city symbolised its annihilation. In a condensation of the story of Troy, Propertius portrays the ploughing as done by the famed wooden horse, which had enabled the Greeks to infiltrate the city. Minerva, goddess of carpentry, helped build the horse.

Callimachus...Philitas: See notes to II.1 and II.34.

My youth: Propertius was probably in his early thirties when Book Three was published. A Roman man was considered a *'iuuenis'* (youth) until the age of about forty.

If you showed the way...: As in II.1, Propertius declares himself ready in theory to write on Greek mythology and Roman history, but now makes this contingent on Maecenas adopting a high-profile position, which he knows will not happen. The war between the gods and the giants was also mentioned in II.1. Cattle grazing on the Palatine Hill, which would become Rome's historical centre, signify the pre-history of the city. Remus was killed by his brother Romulus when he derisively jumped over the nascent walls of Rome, which Romulus was building. Propertius then goes backwards in time to speak of the suckling of the twins by a she-wolf.

Parthians' crafty flight: See note to II.10.

Egyptian bastions: Propertius refers to the capture of Pelusium in the Nile delta, which in fact was not stormed but surrendered to Octavian in 30 BC.

Antony's death: Mark Antony committed suicide at Alexandria in 30 BC following his defeat by Octavian at Actium the previous year.

III.10

Niobe's rock: See note to II.20.

Halcyons ... nightingale: Propertius refers to two bird-related Greek myths. In one, Alcyone's husband died in a shipwreck, and when his body was washed ashore, she was transformed into a halcyon, or kingfisher, to fly to meet him. The other relates how Procne was married to King Tereus and bore him a son named Itys, but when Tereus raped her sister Philomela, the two women killed Itys and served him as food for Tereus. When he realised what had happened he pursued them, but all three were changed into birds: Tereus into a hoopoe, and the sisters into a nightingale and a swallow. Ancient writers portrayed the nightingale's song as a lament for Itys.

III.11

While moving a step closer to 'regime poetry', Propertius still feels it necessary to preface adulation of Augustus with the perfunctory context of a love poem introducing the theme of female power, from the strong heroines of Greek mythology to Cleopatra.

Medea: See also notes to II.4 and II.16b. In order to help Jason take the Golden Fleece from her homeland, she used her magic powers to enable him to yoke fire-breathing bulls and sow the ground with dragon's teeth, from which armed men sprang. She also lulled the dragon that guarded the fleece.

Penthesilea: An Amazon queen from the northern coast of the Black Sea who fought at Troy and was killed by Achilles. When he saw her beauty after her death, he fell in love with her.

Omphale: Queen of Lydia in Asia Minor, with whom Hercules fell in love. She forced him to serve as her slave, wear women's clothing and spin wool. Propertius refers to what is now Lake Marmara in western Turkey, linking it with the nearby gold-bearing Pactolus River (see note to I.6) to imply that her beauty came from its waters. The Pillars of Hercules are the rocks of Gibraltar and Ceuta on either side of the Straits of Gibraltar, portrayed as victory monuments set up by Hercules to mark his liberation of the world from monsters.

Semiramis: Queen of Nineveh, in what is now Iraq, in the ninth century BC. She turns up in Dante's *Inferno* as a woman guilty of lust.

Jupiter: The king of the gods' philandering is further proof of the power of women.

Him who blotted...: Mark Antony.

That Woman: Cleopatra, whose actual name, commentators note, is never used by Augustan poets. Propertius' description of her as '*trita*' (literally 'worn out' but with a clear sexual connotation) by her male slaves is the closest the poet comes to obscene language in any of his extant poems. Her Ptolemaic dynasty in Egypt was descended from the kings of Macedon, best known of whom were Philip and Alexander (the Great). She had a relationship with Julius Caesar, producing a son, and was living in Rome when he was assassinated in 44 BC. Her later famous liaison with Antony resulted in three children. Her son by Julius, Caesarion, was proclaimed pharaoh after her death in 30 BC, but was quickly killed on Augustus' orders, after which Egypt became a Roman province. Cleopatra was thus effectively the last pharaoh. Propertius' rhetoric about her supposed hopes of imposing Egyptian culture on Rome reads like far-fetched xenophobia, but many Romans will have wondered what would have happened had Antony defeated Octavian in the concluding phase of the Republic's civil wars.

Pompey: Pompey the Great (106–48 BC) became the principal rival of Julius Caesar. The three triumphs Propertius refers to were his victories over the faction supporting Marius (see note to II.1) in Africa in 81 BC, over the forces of Quintus Sertorius, another rival commander, in Spain in 72 BC, and over Mithridates, king of Pontus on the Black Sea, in 65 BC (mentioned later in this poem in a reference to standards captured at the Bosphorus). Pompey was defeated by Caesar at Pharsalus in Greece in 48 BC. He fled to Egypt but was murdered on a boat near the coast. During an attempted reconciliation in 59 BC, Pompey had married Julia, daughter of Caesar, who was thus his father-in-law.

Anubis: A dog-headed Egyptian god.

Tambourine: Propertius refers to the *sistrum*, a rattle employed in the worship of the Egyptian goddess Isis. The instrument is still used by the Ethiopian Orthodox Church and features in the opera *Les Troyens* by the nineteenth-century French composer Hector Berlioz.

Felucca poles: Some commentators have assumed a reference to the barge of Cleopatra made famous in *Antony and Cleopatra*: 'The barge she sat in, like a burnish'd throne / Burn'd on the water.' Shakespeare probably took his description from the *Life of Antony* by the Greek historian Plutarch, writing about a century after Propertius. I have preferred a reference to more humble craft, which seems consistent with the Greek word '*baris*' used by Propertius.

Tarpeian Rock: A crag on Rome's Capitoline Hill, from which traitors were thrown to their deaths. See also note to iv.4.

Tarquin: Tarquinius Superbus (Tarquin the Proud), was the last of Rome's seven kings, driven out in the late sixth century BC, according to tradition, because of his tyrannical behaviour and that of his son.

Sacred asps: Cleopatra reputedly committed suicide by snake-bite in Egypt after she and Antony were defeated by Octavian at Actium.

Such a leader: Augustus.

Scipio: Scipio Africanus ended the Second Punic War against the Carthaginians by finally defeating Hannibal at the Battle of Zama in North Africa in 202 BC. His adoptive grandson Scipio Aemilianus (also dubbed Africanus) defeated Carthage in the Third Punic War and destroyed the city in 146 BC.

Camillus: See note to iii.9.

Syphax: The king of Numidia in North Africa was an ally of Carthage.

Pyrrhus: The king of Epirus (north-west Greece) was defeated by the Romans at Benevento, southern Italy, in 275 BC.

Curtius: According to legend, Marcus Curtius 'leapt on horseback, armed, into a chasm which had opened in the forum, because the soothsayers declared that such a sacrifice would ensure the perpetuity of the Roman state' (Camps).

Decius: There is confusion over which of two men named Publius Decius Mus, father and son, supposedly carried out this feat in the fourth or third century BC, and which battle was involved.

Horatius: The Roman hero who 'kept the bridge', as immortalised in the most famous of the *Lays of Ancient Rome* by Thomas Macaulay (1800–59). According to the story, Horatius Cocles defended the western approach to the Sublician Bridge over the Tiber against an attacking Etruscan army in 508 BC. While he held off the enemy, Roman soldiers destroyed the bridge behind him, thus saving the city. The wounded Horatius managed to swim back across the river.

Corvinus: Marcus Valerius received this additional name after a crow ('*coruus*' in Latin) perched on his helmet and harried a Gaul he was fighting during a battle in 348 BC.

Levkas: Propertius is apparently referring to a temple of Apollo on the Greek island of Levkas, from which the flight of Cleopatra's and Antony's ships after the Battle of Actium would have been visible.

One day's war: Heyworth & Morwood say the phrase 'implies that a single day has not only brought warfare to an end; it has destroyed the potential for military epic. All that is possible now is the composition of Augustan panegyric.'

III.12

Postumus: Postumus and Galla were common names in ancient Rome. Some have seen a possible reference to Caius Propertius Postumus, a politician of the day who may have been a relative of the poet. At all events, Propertius, after his encomium for Augustus in the previous poem, here returns to a favourite theme – the superiority of the life of love to military adventures. He will develop the theme of the abandoned military wife at greater length in IV.3.

Parthian spoils: See note to II.10.

Gold-diggers: Propertius takes it as read that the motives for going on campaign included not just glory but self-enrichment from captured booty.

Aras: A river known in ancient times as the Araxes, flowing through what are now Turkey, Armenia, Azerbaijan and Iran.

Ten years' war: There follows a rapid summary of the *Odyssey*, although Ulysses' adventures on the way back from Troy are not listed exactly in Homer's order. Ulysses began by capturing the town of **Ismara** in Thrace, northeastern Greece, and slaughtering the **Cicones**, a people who lived there. He and his men later burnt out with a heated staff the single eye of the **Cyclops** Polyphemus, who had taken them captive. Elsewhere, he dallied with the witch **Circe** and evaded the influence of the **lotus**, a fruit that took away the will to travel on. For **Scylla** and **Charybdis**, see note to II.26b. The nymph **Lampetie** was a daughter of the Sun god, whose cattle she tended. Ulysses' hungry men sacrilegiously killed the animals, which continued to low even when being roasted. On **Calypso**, see note to I.15. Ulysses swam through the sea for two days and nights after being shipwrecked, and also visited the land of the dead in the far west of the world. He stopped up the ears of his crewmen with wax to prevent them being lured to their doom by the music of the **Sirens**. He finally made it home to the island of Ithaca, where he killed the **suitors** who had been wooing his wife **Penelope**.

III.13

Indian miner-ants: The fifth-century-BC Greek historian Herodotus reported that in India giant ants dug up gold-rich sand from the desert.

Tyre: See note to II.16b. The expensive dye was extracted from a vein of the whelk, a type of shellfish.

Felicitous funeral law: The Indian practice of *suttee*, in which a widow threw herself onto her husband's burning funeral pyre, and which only died out in the nineteenth century, was a source of fascination for Roman writers.

Evadne: See note to I.15.

Seeing goddesses naked: The reference is to myths like that of the hunter Actaeon, who stumbled on the goddess Diana bathing in the nude, was changed by her into a stag and was torn to pieces by his own hounds.

'Out for hares...': The next four lines are a fairly close translation of an epigram by Leonidas of Taranto, who wrote in Greek in southern Italy in the third century BC.

Pan: See note to I.18.

Brennus: Leader of the Gauls who attacked the temple of Apollo at Delphi in 278 BC. The implication is that he was driven by love of booty. Ancient writers say the attackers were overwhelmed by a blizzard, although Propertius suggests some kind of landslip caused by an earth tremor.

Polymestor: King Priam of Troy, foreseeing the fall of the city, sent his youngest son Polydorus to King Polymestor of Thrace for safety, along with a quantity of gold. Polymestor seized the gold and killed Polydorus.

Amphiaraus...Eriphyla: See notes to II.16b and II.34.

Cassandra: Daughter of Priam. In an attempt to seduce her, Apollo gave her the gift of prophecy, but when she rebuffed him, he decreed that her (correct) predictions would never be believed. The **horse** is the Trojan Horse, mentioned also in III.9, left as a 'gift' to Troy but full of Greek warriors who stormed the city when it was rolled inside.

III.14

Sparta: Ancient Sparta, in the Greek Peloponnese, was a militaristic society. But under statutes attributed to the legendary lawgiver Lycurgus, women were said to enjoy greater equality with men than did their sisters in other Greek cities, such as Athens. According to ancient writers, this included them taking part in sports – in the nude, as men did (the Greek word '*gymnos*', root of our 'gymnasium', means 'naked'). Propertius was not the only male classical author to fantasise about this notion, which was picked up in more recent times by Edgar Degas in his 1860 painting *Young Spartans*

Exercising. The aim of the practice, however, seems to have been to help women produce healthy sons to serve in the army. Praise of women's athletics is expanded in the poem into general acclamation of what Propertius says was Sparta's more free-and-easy relationship between the sexes than that in first-century-BC Rome. Scholars are divided on whether young Spartan women really did exercise naked, or at least semi-naked. One recent discussion, by Francis Cairns, concludes that the idea 'cannot be dismissed as impossible' and that Propertius' description of women's status in general 'sticks fairly closely to ancient belief about Sparta and indeed to the facts'.

Amazons: These mythical female warriors were reputed to come from around the River Thermodon, now the Terme, which flows into the Black Sea in northern Turkey. Propertius depicts them as bare-breasted but does not mention the story that they had one breast removed to enable them to draw their bows more easily.

Taygetus, Eurotas: Respectively, a mountain and a river near Sparta.

Castor and Pollux: In mythology, twin sons of Leda, wife of Spartan King Tyndareus (see also note to 1.13). Castor was a noted horseman, Pollux a pugilist. Their sister was Helen (of Troy). The Greek myths differ as to which of Leda's children were sired by Tyndareus and which by the god Jupiter.

III.15

Boyhood clothing: At the age of around seventeen, upper-class Roman boys gave up the purple-edged '*toga praetexta*' in favour of the plain white '*toga virilis*'.

Lycinna: After insisting from the start of Book One that Cynthia was 'first', Propertius (that is, the figure portrayed in the poems, not necessarily the historical man) now reveals that he actually lost his virginity to another woman. The name is not found elsewhere in his work, but suggests a slave-girl. He speaks of her with affection, while maintaining that Cynthia was his only real love.

Dirce ... Antiope: The convoluted myth of Antiope would have been familiar to readers from a play by Euripides, small parts of which survive today. She was the daughter of Nycteus, a king in the Greek region of Boeotia, her beauty catching the attention of Jupiter, who made her pregnant. She gave birth to twin boys, Zethus and Amphion, leaving them on Mount Cithaeron, near Thebes, where they were brought up by a shepherd. Angry at her behaviour, her dying father asked his brother, Lycus, to punish her, leading to her being taken as a slave by Lycus' wife, Dirce, who maltreated her as recounted by Propertius. Escaping, she made her way to the hut on Cithaeron where her now grown-up sons lived. They at first turned her away, failing to recognise her until the old shepherd intervened. The sons then killed the pursuing Dirce by tying her to the horns of a bull (a massive Hellenistic sculpture of the dramatic scene is kept at the National Archaeological Museum in Naples). The poem only makes sense, however, under a version of the myth in which Antiope also had a previous relationship with Lycus, explaining Dirce's antipathy to her, which is compared to Cynthia's jealousy of Lycinna.

Amphion: His lyre-playing is also mentioned in 1.9 – qv and note.

Aracynthus: Another mountain near Thebes.

III.16

White-roofed towers: Propertius' *'geminas turres'* translates literally as 'twin towers' – a phrase hopelessly compromised since September 11, 2001. I have taken it to denote buildings on either side of the Aniene falls, with their 100-metre drop, in the beauty spot of Tivoli, east of Rome. In IV.7, Tivoli is mentioned as Cynthia's burial place.

Sciron: A mythical bandit who lived near the Greek city of Megara. After killing many wayfarers by pushing them over a cliff, he was eventually dealt with in similar fashion by Theseus.

Scythia: The area north of the Black Sea, often used by the Romans to denote a distant, foreign land inhabited by dangerous barbarians.

III.17

This poem, which has been interpreted as one of several (others are III.21 and III.23) building up to the 'final' farewell to Cynthia (and by implication to love poetry) in III.24–25, is cast as a hymn to Bacchus. Hymns were common in classical poetry, and Roman readers will perhaps have recalled the one to the same deity in Sophocles' *Antigone*, where the chorus pleads for Thebes' salvation. Many scholars, however, have detected irony, even humour, in Propertius' version – in the end, all he asks for is alcoholic oblivion from his affair with Cynthia. Others have detected a more serious purpose, suggesting he wanted to reclaim for Augustus a god who had been adopted as a sponsor by Mark Antony, as well as to promote viticulture.

Ariadne: See also notes to 1.3 and II.3. After Bacchus rescued her from Naxos (the island is mentioned later in the poem), he took her 'to heaven as his bride, and made her crown into a constellation' (Camps).

Lightning bolts: Bacchus was born prematurely when his mother Semele was burnt up after persuading her lover Jupiter to appear to her in his full effulgence (see note to II.28). He was saved by being sewn into Jupiter's thigh until his term was due. Later he travelled in the east with his followers, who put to flight all opponents.

Lycurgus: A Thracian king who opposed worship of Bacchus. He was driven mad, cut off his own legs and killed his son, thinking he was chopping down vines.

Pentheus: Another foe of Bacchus who came to grief, as recounted in Euripides' *Bacchae*. He was torn to pieces by his mother and aunts, who had become maenads.

Tendrilled vessel: 'Bacchus in human form was travelling on a ship, and the crew plotted to sell him as a slave. When he disclosed himself, the sailors went mad and leapt into the sea, becoming dolphins, and the ship was suddenly overgrown with vines.' (Camps).

I'll drape you ...: Propertius' pledge to promote worship of Bacchus dwells on the oriental and effeminate (the two concepts were synonymous to Romans) aspect of the god. **Cybele** was a mother-goddess whose cult originated in Anatolia but was imported to Italy at the end of the third century BC. She was also identified as a defender of cities and was depicted in ancient art with a mural crown.

Pindar: The great Greek lyric poet (518–438 BC), best known for his still extant odes celebrating victors in the Olympic and other Panhellenic games. This is another of Propertius' promises to adopt a loftier tone in future.

III.18

An elegy for Marcus Claudius Marcellus, son of Augustus' sister Octavia. He married the emperor's daughter, his first cousin Julia, and was seen as heir apparent, but fell ill and died in Baia, on the Gulf of Naples, in 23 BC at the age of nineteen. His death is also treated in a passage of the *Aeneid*, which, when Vergil recited it at the imperial court, is said to have caused Octavia to faint. The name of Marcellus does not appear in the transmitted Latin text, but would have been obvious to Propertius' audience. I have inserted it in the translation to help the modern reader.

Averno: Apparently another reference to the port built by Augustus' lieutenant Agrippa, which allowed the sea into Lake Averno, an area also renowned for being a portal to the underworld. See, in general, the note to I.11. There, Baia is denounced as a place where Cynthia is likely to be unfaithful; here as the site of Marcellus' death. There is also a reference to Baia's volcanic springs.

Aeneas' trumpeter: Misenus, who fell to his death from cliffs at Cuma after challenging the sea-god Triton to a trumpeting competition, as mentioned in the *Aeneid*. The headland at the north-west end of the Gulf of Naples is still called Cape Miseno.

Hercules' road: See note to I.11.

Bacchus: A trip to Italy by the wine-god is mentioned only by Propertius.

Crowd at the stadium: Shortly before his death, Marcellus had staged spectacular games in Rome.

Dog's mouths: A reference to the underworld hound Cerberus. See note to III.5. The **grim greybeard** is Charon, who ferried dead souls across the Styx.

Nireus: Famed as the most handsome of the Greeks who went to Troy.

Pactolus: See note to I.6. The river's gold contributed to the fabled wealth of the Lydian king Croesus.

The sailor: Presumably a further reference to Charon. But these closing lines take us to the limits of our knowledge of Roman eschatology. The one thing that seems clear is that the poet hopes Marcellus will follow the path of Julius Caesar, who was believed by the populace to have become a god when a comet appeared in the sky a few months after his assassination in 44 BC. Propertius, alone among Roman authors, attributes the same destiny to Marcellus' ancestor, Claudius Marcellus, who had captured Syracuse in Sicily for Rome during the war with Hannibal in 211 BC. But scholars are divided – and have emended the text accordingly – on whether the poet is praying that Marcellus' body will go to the Elysian Fields in the underworld, and his soul to heaven, or vice versa. I have followed the latter interpretation.

III.19

Sirt: The name of what is now a Libyan city was applied in ancient times to dangerous offshore sandbanks. *Malea*, on the southern tip of the Peloponnese, in Greece, was also a notorious graveyard of shipping.

Her whose love …: Pasiphae, on whom see note to II.28.

Tyro: See note to I.13.

Medea: See also notes to II.4, II.16b and III.11. In the famous drama by Euripides, Medea, abandoned by Jason, killed their two sons.

That adultery: After King Agamemnon of Mycenae left for the Trojan War, his wife Clytemnestra took Aegisthus as a lover. Together, they murdered Agamemnon on his return.

Myrrha: A Cypriot princess who deceived her father into incest. While fleeing his wrath she was turned into a myrrh tree.

Scylla: This final mythological example of female sexual perversion records how King Minos of Crete attacked the mainland Greek city of Megara. Its king, Nisus, was kept safe by a magic lock of purple hair, but his daughter

Scylla, enamoured of Minos, cut it off, causing Nisus' death and the fall of the city. Instead of rewarding her, Minos tied her to the stern of his ship and dragged her to her death in the sea for treachery to her father. Propertius says that because of this act of justice, Minos was rightly appointed after his death to be a judge of the underworld (where he shows up, in monstrous form, in Dante).

III.20

The poem purports to be written to a woman whose boyfriend has dumped her to take up a lucrative assignment in the province of Africa, presumably on Roman government service. The writer offers himself as a replacement. Some have found the transition to a discourse on the need for a relationship contract to be too abrupt and proposed to split the poem in two. There has also been much debate on whether the addressee is Cynthia (who is not named in the poem, but then neither is she in several others generally acknowledged to be addressed to her) or to another woman. A majority of recent commentators have inclined to the second view, largely because Propertius talks of a 'new' relationship, hardly appropriate for Cynthia near the end of his third book of verse about her.

The skills of chaste Minerva: Ovid lists the accomplishments of the goddess Minerva as including learning, spinning, weaving, dyeing, shoemaking, carpentry, medicine, teaching, sculpture and painting.

A learned ancestor: This phrase has set the literary historiographers off on a trail of speculation. Some have said it proves the recipient is not Cynthia, who is portrayed in some poems as a courtesan and therefore unlikely to have had a distinguished ancestor. Others have said that if Apuleius was correct in identifying Cynthia as a certain Hostia (see Afterword), then the second-century-BC poet Hostius could have been her ancestor.

Ariadne's starry crown: See note to III.17.

III.21

Grand tour to Athens: The idea of foreign travel to get away from a love affair is an established one in classical literature. But Athens was indeed a frequent destination for young upper-class Romans, thanks to its traditions of philosophy, culture and art, recalling the role played by the 'grand tour' to Italy for well-to-do Englishmen in the eighteenth and nineteenth centuries. There is no other evidence that Propertius visited Athens and his avowed intention to do so is more likely simply to prepare the reader for the farewell poem III.24–25. His pledge to improve himself with the study of Greek philosophers, orators and playwrights during a stay possibly lasting years is hard to take at face value. The ironic tone is very different from the anguish of Catullus' 'it's over' in Poem 8.

Turn of marine deities: Instead of the love deities Propertius has hitherto prayed to.

Corinth port: A journey to Athens would have involved a sea voyage to Corinth, then (the Corinth canal having not yet been constructed) land travel across the isthmus to the port on the eastern side where the traveller would again have boarded ship to reach Piraeus – then, as now, the port for Athens, some seven miles away.

Epicurus: The Greek philosopher (341–270 BC) taught that pleasure was the highest good, but also attacked the idea of love as a serious emotion. His theories had recently formed the basis of the Roman writer Lucretius' scientific poem *De rerum natura* (On the Nature of the Universe).

Demosthenes: Regarded as the greatest of the Greek orators, he lived from 384–322 BC. His political speeches aimed mainly to counter the southward expansion of the kingdom of Macedonia, and we still have the word 'philippic' to remind us of his tirades against Philip of Macedon. Demosthenes' efforts ultimately failed and he committed suicide rather than be apprehended by Macedonian representatives.

Menander: The master of Greek 'new comedy' (see also note to II.6). His refined plays contrast with the rumbustious and often rude fantasies of 'old comedy', as seen in the extant plays of Aristophanes.

III.22

Cyzicus: A once important town on what was originally an island of the same name in the Sea of Marmara but later became a peninsula, now known as Kapidag and located in Turkey. Ruined by a series of earthquakes in the Middle Ages, the town survives as an archaeological site. The nearest modern city is Erdek.

Tullus: His first appearance since Book One, where he was introduced (see notes to I.1 and I.6) as Propertius' dedicatee. Evidently he stayed for years in Asia Minor for reasons we can only guess at. Here, Propertius appeals to him to come home and pursue the career of the typical upper-class Roman, but the tone is hard to gauge. The praise of Italy echoes passages of Vergil's *Georgics* and *Aeneid*, but some critics have suggested parody. We do not know how Tullus reacted, and nothing further is heard of him.

Cybele: See note to III.17. Cyzicus was one of several places associated with her cult.

Pluto: Known to the Romans as Dis, the king of the underworld famously abducted Persephone (or Proserpina) to be his bride, an event more commonly located in Sicily.

Cayster: A river a little further south in western Turkey, now called the Küçük Menderes.

Maeander: See note to II.30.

Atlas: Depicted as a giant who supported the sky on his shoulders, and identified with the Atlas Mountains in what is now Morocco. This is the first of a series of potential sights set in the west of the then known world.

Medusa: The Gorgon's face turned people to stone (so hardly something Tullus would want to look at), but Perseus slew her using his shield as a mirror.

Geryon: A three-bodied king living on an island beyond the Straits of Gibraltar (and another classical monster who appears in Dante's *Inferno*). Hercules killed him and seized his oxen as one of his labours. The next two references are also to Hercules, who out-wrestled the giant **Antaeus** in Libya and stole golden apples from the garden of **Hesperus' daughters**, guarded by a dragon, in the far west (see note to II.24b).

Colchis: Propertius now turns his attention to the east, with the voyage of the Argo to the Black Sea.

Rocks: The Symplegades – see note to II.26b.

Controlled anger in victory: Propertius' odd phrase '*victrices temperat ira manus*' (literally, 'anger tempers our hands when they are victorious') leads Heyworth & Morwood to cite Aeneas' killing of Turnus at the close of the *Aeneid*, which, they say, 'gives a remarkable picture of the man who symbolizes Rome rejecting restraint out of anger … The confusion of the *Aeneid*'s moral message is thus encapsulated in the Propertian phrase.'

Marcius' … aqueduct: See note to III.2.

Albano, Nemi: Lakes in the hills south of Rome.

Wholesome spring: The Lake of Juturna in the Roman Forum. Castor and Pollux were said to have watered their horses there after – according to legend – helping the Romans beat off an attempt by the Tarquins to reclaim the city's throne at the (historical) Battle of Lake Regillus in the early fifth century BC.

Andromeda: See note to I.3. There follows a series of other unpleasant episodes in Greek mythology, things Propertius says do not happen in Italy. The **banquets** refer to how King Atreus of Mycenae killed the sons of his brother Thyestes and served them to him at a feast – an incident that caused the disgusted Sun-god to turn back in his tracks. The **death sentences** recall how the Fates told the warrior Meleager's mother Althaea that he would live as long as a log burning on her hearth. She removed the log and hid it, but when Meleager later killed her brothers she burnt it, causing his death. On the **Bacchae**, see note to III.17. Pentheus' killers tore him from a tree where he had taken refuge. The **substituted deer** relates to the story of Iphigenia, who was ordered to be sacrificed by her father Agamemnon to stop unfavourable winds blocking the departure of the Greek fleet for Troy. In one version, a hind was substituted for her at the last moment and she escaped. **Juno** is yet another reference to the myth of Io, on which see note to I.3.

III.23

Writing tablets: Catullus (earlier) and Ovid (later) also wrote light-hearted poems about their writing tablets. These consisted of a double board covered with wax, with raised wooden surrounds and hinged so they could be folded shut and sealed. Propertius says that even without his personal seal, his tablets could be easily recognised. He suggests that he used them both to compose poetry and to exchange messages with girlfriends. Some scholars have surmised that the poem, which speaks of multiple women and does not mention Cynthia, is to prepare the reader for the next poem's formal dismissal of her.

The Esquiline: Propertius says again in IV.8 that he lived on Rome's Esquiline Hill (not far today from the city's main railway station), which was also the area where Maecenas resided.

III.24–25

Cast as Propertius' final farewell to Cynthia. But she appears again in IV.7 (as a ghost) and IV.8 (alive).

Aegean waters: The Aegean Sea has been noted since ancient times for its storms.

Thessaly: See note to I.5. The reference to magic is probably a deliberate echo of I.1, as this poem purports to close off a chapter opened by Propertius' first published work.

IV.1

I read IV.1 as a single poem, as in the manuscripts, though some editors print it as two, the second beginning with Horos' intervention half-way through (after the asterisks in my version). Scholars have long argued the point. Neither side seems to me to have made a conclusive case, but on balance I prefer to see this as a more elaborate version of III.3, where Propertius is talked out of a plan to write historical epic.

Palatine: One of the seven hills on which Rome was built, it overlooks the Forum. Propertius begins the poem in the guise (soon dropped) of a tourist guide.

Evander: In Roman mythology, a semi-divine figure from the Greek region of Arcadia who brought Greek culture to Italy, founding the city of Pallanteum on the future site of Rome before the Trojan War and instituting the Lupercalia festival, mentioned further on in this poem. He figures prominently in Vergil's *Aeneid*.

Tarpeian rock: See also notes to III.11 and IV.4. In Propertius' day it was the site of a temple to Jupiter Capitolinus, but he is saying this was not always so.

Immigrant Tiber: An apparent reference to the fact that the river flowed down from what was then Etruria. Its source is in what is now the Italian region of Emilia-Romagna.

Romulus' home: The house of the founder of Rome and his twin brother Remus was another site that had been greatly developed from humble origins.

Vesta: See also notes to II.29b and III.4. 'At the Vestalia on 9 June both cornmills and the donkeys that worked them were garlanded with flowers and the donkeys had loaves of bread hung around their necks.' (Camps).

Lupercalia: In Propertius' time, the festival was held on 15 February. Selected young men ran around the Palatine striking with goat-skin thongs any woman they came across, in a ritual supposed to promote fertility. The practice is mentioned in Shakespeare's *Julius Caesar*, where Caesar instructs Mark Antony, who will be one of the runners, to strike his (Caesar's) wife Calpurnia, in the hope that she will conceive.

Lycmon: An Etruscan king who helped Romulus against Titus *Tatius*, king of the Sabines. Tatius later ruled Rome jointly with Romulus. He is dealt with at length in IV.4.

Bovillae ... Gabii ... Alba ... Fidene: Four once significant towns near Rome that by Propertius' day had either been absorbed into the conurbation or disappeared. On Alba, see note to III.3. The only place that still survives is Fidene, now a Rome suburb.

Troy: Propertius develops the theme, central to the *Aeneid*, that although the Greeks sacked Troy, the escape of Aeneas and his followers, resulting eventually in the rise of Rome, represented the survival of Troy and even its revenge upon Greece. Propertius makes much of the Roman concept of

Penates, or household gods, which came to be synonymous with a home. They are seen as having existed in Troy and been brought to Italy by Aeneas.

Trembling father: Anchises, who, in the legend, was carried out of Troy on the shoulders of his son, Aeneas.

Decius: See note to III.11.

Brutus: Not the assassin of Caesar, but his supposed ancestor Lucius Junius Brutus, who overthrew the Tarquin kings in 509 BC and became one of Rome's first consuls. The reference to his axes is ambiguous: they were the symbol of consular authority but were also used to execute criminals. Brutus had his own sons executed for conspiring against the state.

Her progeny Caesar: See note to III.4. In the *Aeneid*, Vergil portrays Venus as using her bedroom skills to persuade her husband Vulcan, the smith-god, to make new armour for Aeneas.

Julus: The son of Aeneas.

Sibyl: See also note to II.2. She was said to have resided at Cuma, near Lake Averno (see also note to I.11) in the Naples area. Propertius suggests that she forecast the death of Remus – slain by his brother for derisively jumping over the nascent walls of Rome – as a ritual sacrifice that would ensure the city's future prosperity.

Cassandra: See note to III.13.

Ennius: See note to III.3. By appealing to Bacchus for a wreath of his ivy, Propertius is implicitly contrasting himself with a poet seen by his time as venerable, but antiquated and uncouth.

Whoa!: The speaker for the rest of the poem, aside from a sub-quotation attributed to Apollo, is Horos, an astrologer who is otherwise unknown but whose name presumably recalls the word 'horoscope'. Some of his speech seems intended to suggest astrological mumbo-jumbo, but the overall purpose, I would argue, is once again to use humour as a way to deflect the pressure on Propertius to write 'regime poetry', instead continuing to use the elegiac-couplet metre that was considered incompatible with epic.

Archytas: A Greek polymath (428–347 BC) of the Pythagorean school, whose specialities included astronomy. **Orops** is unknown and possibly invented by Propertius, though the name suggests the Middle East. **Conon**, from the Greek island of Samos, was a third-century-BC astronomer and mathematician, known for having named the Lock of Berenice constellation.

Capricorn: The constellation sets below the western horizon, hence, from the Roman standpoint, in the sea.

Arria ... Lupercus ... Gallus: All unknown. Commentators believe, however, that the reference may be to the 'Lollius disaster', in which Roman legions under the control of Marcus Lollius, governor of Gaul, were defeated by German tribes that had crossed the Rhine in 16 BC (approximate date of Book Four).

Cinara: Also unknown. Juno Lucina was the goddess of childbirth.

Jupiter's sandy cave: An oracle of a North African version of Jupiter at the Siwa oasis in Libya. In attempting to foresee the future, the ancients attached much importance to birds – their calls (as mentioned earlier in the poem), their flight and their entrails. Our word 'auspicious' derives from Latin '*auspicium*', meaning 'observation of birds'. Propertius' reference to spirits rising from bowls of water reminds us that the modern practices of mediums have a long history.

Five zones: In his *Georgics*, Vergil, following the third-century-BC Greek geographer Eratosthenes, speaks of five zones of the sky (and hence of earth) – two cold, two temperate and one hot.

Calchas: The mythological seer who said that in order to turn the winds that were holding the Troy-bound Greek fleet at Aulis, Agamemnon's daughter Iphigenia would have to be sacrificed (see also note to III.22).

Nauplius: See note to II.26b.

The prophetess: A further reference to Cassandra, who, after the fall of Troy, was raped by a Greek fighter known as Ajax the Lesser (to distinguish him from the mighty warrior Ajax, subject of a play by Sophocles).

The Umbrian lake: A modern reader familiar with Italy might take this to be Trasimeno, the country's fourth largest lake. Some scholars agree, but others say that in Roman times Trasimeno was in Etruria, not Umbria, and that Propertius must be referring to another lake presumed to have existed near Assisi but to have since dried up.

Bailiff's rod: This section is our primary evidence for believing that at least part of the Propertius family estate in Umbria was taken away to provide farmland for Octavian's veterans (see note to I.21). It accounts for most of our scanty knowledge of the poet's early life, including that he rejected a legal career. In their mid-teens, Roman boys gave up an amulet, or locket, normally donated by their fathers, and began to wear an adult male's toga.

'Write love poems…': The next twelve lines are ascribed by editors to Apollo, quoted by Horos.

Her boys: The Cupids, often seen (as in II.29a) as a group rather than an individual.

One girl: Clearly, Cynthia. Propertius serves notice that, despite the apparent final farewell in III.24–25, she is not forgotten. She will, in fact, reappear in IV.7 and IV.8.

The eight-footed Crab: The bizarre end to the poem may be intended as more astrological hokum. Scholars have, however, found one or two mentions in classical authors of the star-sign Cancer being inimical to lovers. Some have suggested that, because coins dating from the period of Book Four have been found with a crab design on the back, Horos may be advising Propertius to beware the power of money – or of Augustus, who appeared on the obverse.

IV.2

Vertumnus: Much of what we know about this Etruscan deity derives from this poem, in which he is the speaker. He is mentioned by other Roman authors, though, including the historian and agricultural writer Varro, a rough contemporary of Propertius, who called him 'the chief god of Etruria'. Associated with the seasons and the harvest, Vertumnus had a statue – Propertius says originally of wood but later of bronze – in the Vicus Tuscus ('Tuscan Street', mentioned later in this poem), which came to the Forum from the Tiber under the slopes of the Palatine. Part of the poem deals with the origin of the god's name, which, in the line arrangement adopted here, he links with the battle soon after Rome's foundation (traditionally in 753 BC) when the allied Romans and Etruscans (see note to IV.1) defeated the Sabines. The poem as we have it, however, does not make clear the name's true etymology.

Old Tiber: The district known as the Velabro, where the Vicus Tuscus ran, was originally marshy, with overspill from the Tiber. It was later drained, in what Propertius describes as a benevolent act by the river.

Numa: Numa Pompilius was the second king of Rome, succeeding Romulus, according to Roman historians, who give the dates of his reign as 715–673 BC.

Mamurrius: Mamurrius Veturius was a legendary sculptor in early Rome. He came from Campania, to the south.

IV.3

Styx-water: See note to II.9. Arethusa is saying with heavy irony that all the customary rituals at her wedding must have been blighted by ill omens, since her husband now spends so much time away from home.

Ocnus: '[A] proverbial character who let an extravagant wife waste the fruits of his industry, and was condemned to sit to eternity twisting (i.e. making) a rope, while a donkey standing by ate it up ... as fast as he made it.' (Camps).

Tyrian wool: See note to II.16b.

Aras River: See note to III.12.

Parthian camels: See note to II.10.

Hippolyte: Leader of the Amazons, on whom see note to III.14.

Sabine herbs: The Sabine hills lie north and east of Rome. Arethusa says she has observed all necessary religious rituals to ensure Lycotas' safe return. A hooting owl was considered to herald bad luck. But, according to Ovid, a sputtering lamp was a good omen, to which the correct response was to sprinkle it with drops of wine. Both good and bad omens would have required animal sacrifices, arranged – for payment – by assistant priests.

Conqueror's spear: A victorious commander carried an untipped spear in his triumphal procession.

Capena Gate: At the start of the Appian Way, which headed south-east out of Rome. The Senate consecrated an altar there to mark Augustus' return from the East in 19 BC.

IV.4

The name of the Tarpeian Rock, on the Capitoline Hill, derived from Tarpeia, a Vestal Virgin who betrayed the hill to the Sabines attacking Rome in reprisal for the Rape of the Sabine Women, an event traditionally dated to 750 BC during the reign of Romulus (see also below and note to II.6; the Roman-Sabine conflict has already been mentioned in IV.1 and IV.2). The Vestal Virgins (on whom see also notes to II.29b and III.4) were chosen before puberty and served for thirty years. They received significant privileges but also faced severe penalties for wrongdoing. The punishment for letting Vesta's fire go out was scourging. If they had sexual relations with men they could be buried alive (there are ten reported cases of this in the thousand years or so during which the office continued). Because of Tarpeia's role as a Vestal, her treachery is portrayed as particularly heinous. Her tomb no longer existed in Propertius' day.

Cures: A Sabine city, where Passo Corese is now sited, from which Tatius launched his campaign.

Silvanus: A rural deity.

Scylla: See note to III.19. But Propertius here blends that Scylla, whose story resembles that of Tarpeia, with the monster of the same name at the Straits of Messina (see note to II.26b), whose lower parts were portrayed as ravening hounds.

Ariadne: See note to I.3. She was the daughter of Pasiphae and King Minos, while the Minotaur was the offspring of Pasiphae and a bull, making Ariadne its half-sister. She gave Theseus a ball of thread to help him escape, after killing the monster, from the labyrinth where it was kept.

Minerva's fire: An image of Minerva, said to have come from Troy, was kept in the temple of Vesta.

Motherless child: Romulus. His mother was in fact the princess Rhea Silvia, but he was abandoned, along with his twin brother Remus, to die in the flooding Tiber; the river receded and they were rescued by a she-wolf.

Rape of the Sabine Women: The phrase has passed into history. But I have not followed some other translators in rendering Propertius' arresting Latin '*me rape*' in the next line as 'rape me' – on the grounds that, as mentioned in the note to II.6, the Latin term strictly means abduction rather than sexual violation. With '*I can ease apart...*' Tarpeia lays claim to the role Roman historians ascribed to the abducted Sabine women of mediating an end to the war between their Sabine families and new Roman husbands.

Venus: As Aeneas' mother, a partisan of the Trojan and later the Roman cause.

Terme River: See note to III.14. Propertius here seems to merge the bacchants, identified with the Greek region of Thrace, with the Amazons, who lived near the Terme.

Parilia: The feast of Pales, a shepherds' deity, which was celebrated on 21 April, supposed date of the foundation of Rome.

IV.5

The poem is addressed to a *lena* – the female manager of a prostitute. The character was a stock villain of ancient comedy, and the tone of the poem seems primarily comic. The debt to the theatre is recognised in the reference to Menander. We learn late on that the woman's name is Acanthis, related to the Greek word for 'thorn' (thorns are mentioned at the start of the poem). Scholars have dismissed the notion that the 'lady-friend' referred to could be Cynthia. But it is worth noting that some of the tricks Acanthis recommends to her protegée are elsewhere described as characteristic of Cynthia.

Cerberus: See note to III.5.

Hippolytus: See note on *Phaedra* in II.1.

Antinous: Leader of the suitors who besieged Ulysses' wife Penelope during his absence.

Secretions from a mare: In the last of his jibes at Acanthis' supposed witch-like powers, Propertius mentions '*hippomanes*', a substance obtained from mares in heat or pregnant, which ancient writers describe variously as an aphrodisiac or poison (apparently the latter is meant here).

Tyrian dyes: See note to II.16b. I have abbreviated and simplified this section to get rid of some proper names of marginal importance.

Kos: See note to I.2. Its fabrics are referred to again later in the poem as much more valuable than verses from the same place – a reference to Philitas of Kos, one of Propertius' role-models.

Isis time: See note to II.33a for the period of sexual abstinence observed by female devotees of Isis. The significance of April in the next line may be just that it precedes May, when the woman's birthday supposedly falls, but some commentators note that April was sacred to Venus. Birthdays were, of course, reasons for demanding more gifts.

Write ... anything!: The instruction to the prostitute is to pretend to be writing a *billet doux* to another man, to strengthen her bargaining power with the one visiting her.

Menander's pricy Thais: See note to II.6. Acanthis' point is that Medea brought her troubles on herself by asking Jason for love, whereas Thais played hard-to-get.

Some barbarian: The reference is to imported slaves put up for sale in the Forum. Their feet were chalked to show they were foreign, and they might be told to jump to demonstrate their physical fitness. See also II.16b for a resentful reference to former slaves who had won their freedom and made enough money to be able to afford Cynthia's favours.

Scented Paestum: South of Naples. Now much visited for its Greek temples, it was renowned in ancient times for its roses.

IV.6

The Battle of Actium had taken place some fifteen years earlier, but the poem is nominally about the temple (already mentioned in II.31–32, qv) built on the Palatine to Apollo, who is portrayed as the chief actor in the victory.

Philitas ... Cyrenean: Yet another reference to the Hellenistic poets Philitas of Kos and Callimachus of Cyrene, on whom see notes to II.1 and II.34.

A woman: The battle is depicted as against Cleopatra, with no mention of Antony.

Delos: Legend had it that the Aegean island floated until Apollo was born there and fixed it still.

His hair ...: Propertius stresses that Apollo is shedding his normal role as patron of poetry to make war as an archer. The god will reassume his artistic function towards the end of the poem.

Gutting the Greek camp: At the start of Homer's *Iliad*, Apollo sends a plague on the Greek forces at Troy after Agamemnon refuses to hand back Chryseis, daughter of one of the god's priests, whom he had captured.

Python: 'Apollo's first exploit in archery was to kill the snake Python at Delphi' (commentary by Gregory Hutchinson).

Alba Longa: See note to III.3.

Romulus: 'Romulus and Remus took auguries to see who would rule Rome; Romulus, standing on the Palatine, saw twelve birds to Remus' six.' (Hutchinson).

Roman waves: Although Actium was located on the shore of Epirus, northwest Greece, the area had long been controlled by Rome.

Julius: Julius Caesar, adoptive father of Octavian/Augustus, was proclaimed as divine after his assassination in 44 BC (see also note to III.18). A comet that appeared after his death was popularly supposed to be his spirit.

Triton: See note to II.31–32. 'Or hear old Triton blow his wreathèd horn' (William Wordsworth, 'The World Is Too Much With Us').

Jugurtha: See note to III.5.

Falernian: See note to II.33b.

Cilician: From what is now southern Turkey. Commentators say the perfume was made from the saffron plant.

Rhinelanders: The Sygambri, who worsted Roman legions in 16 BC (see also note to IV.1) but soon submitted as Augustus' forces approached.

Ethiopia: Roman expeditions between 24 and 21 BC advanced well into Ethiopia.

Parthians: See note to II.10.

Offspring: Propertius suggests that the diplomatic deal in which the Parthians handed back Crassus' standards was just a temporary ruse by Augustus, and he was leaving a proper defeat of the Middle Eastern people to Gaius (born 20 BC) and Lucius (born 17 BC) Caesar, sons of his daughter Julia and adopted by him. In the event, both were dead by AD 4 and the Parthians were never conquered.

IV.7

Lethe's water: Lethe, meaning forgetfulness in Greek, was a river of the underworld.

Subura: A racy Rome district noted for its tenement blocks and taverns, and – more to the point here – as a red-light quarter. It was located around what is now the lower part of Via Cavour, below the Esquiline near the Forum. Cynthia conjures up a stock-in-trade of ancient literature, the young woman who escapes from her (usually ageing) husband, client or keeper to be with her lover, but with some characteristic extra Propertian touches.

Lygdamus: See note to III.6. Among the many abuses inflicted on slaves in classical times was the use of torture to extract information. They doubtless also suffered punishments like those visited on the unfortunate Petale and

Lalage, but the whole tone of this section is deliberately over-the-top. Similarly, Cynthia's earlier string of allegations about Propertius' failings at her funeral is intended to sound preposterous.

Nomas: Presumably either another slave in league with Lygdamus or a professional witch who prepared the poison Cynthia claims was used to kill her. The name is Greek, like all the slaves' names in the poem.

Fates: The Fates were portrayed as female deities, spinning the thread of life.

Two destinations: The notion that people are treated in the next life according to their conduct in this one did not start with Dante and has a solid pedigree in ancient literature. Cynthia appears to say at the end of the poem that visions coming from the part of the underworld where the righteous dwell are true.

Clytemnestra, Pasiphae: On Clytemnestra, see note to III.19. For murdering Agamemnon, she was in turn killed by her son Orestes. On Pasiphae, see notes to II.28 and IV.4.

Cybele: See note to III.17.

Andromeda, Hypermnestra: On Andromeda, see note to I.3. On Hypermnestra, see note to II.31–32.

Chloris: Either the ex-prostitute that Cynthia claims is Propertius' new lover or, like Nomas, a specialist in herbal concoctions.

Aniene: See also note to III.16, where Cynthia orders Propertius to visit her in Tivoli. The area's climate was reputed to prevent ivory from discolouring. Hercules was the patron of Tivoli, with a temple there.

The boatman: Charon, on whom see note to III.18.

IV.8

Esquiline: Like the Aventine mentioned later, one of the seven hills on which Rome was built. Propertius also says in III.23 he had a house on the Esquiline, an area now dominated by the basilica of Santa Maria Maggiore. The 'new park' apparently refers to gardens created out of an old cemetery by Maecenas, who lived in the same district.

Lanuvio: Ancient Lanuvium, a town twenty miles south-east of Rome, and the site of a famous temple of Juno. It was reached by the Appian Way, a road that still exists. Propertius jibes that Cynthia was actually going to worship not Juno, as she claimed, but Venus, i.e. for sex with another man (the 'beau' who is described in slighting terms).

Gladiator: Contrary to its modern image, the gladiator's profession was considered the lowest form of employment in Propertius' day.

Magnus: If the manuscript reading is correct, an ironic name for a dwarf who performs a sort of freak-show in the entertainment laid on by Propertius for his two guests.

Dice: Four dice were used. The highest throw (1, 3, 4, 6) was called 'Venus', the lowest (1, 1, 1, 1) was 'the dog'.

Pompey's Portico ... the Forum: Pick-up locations in ancient Rome.

IV.9

The Ara Maxima (literally 'Biggest Altar'), the earliest cult centre of Hercules in Rome, was closed to female worshippers. It was built in 495 BC between the Palatine and the Tiber – possibly on the site of an earlier shrine – where the church of Santa Maria in Cosmedin currently stands. Propertius may be following the historian Varro in attributing the rule to the legend that Hercules was once denied water by a female religious community on the Aventine.

The bullocks: One of the labours of Hercules (see note to II.24b) was to seize the cattle of the giant Geryon, who lived on the mythical island of Erythea, beyond the Straits of Gibraltar.

Velabro: See note to IV.2.

Cacus: The implication is that Cacus, as a local resident, owed a debt of hospitality to the traveller Hercules. Propertius, unlike other Latin authors, depicts Cacus with three heads – possibly an echo of the triple-headed Geryon. His cave is described as 'menacing' and 'horrible' perhaps because, as some ancient writers relate, he decorated it with the bones of his victims.

Forum Bovarium: (Also Boarium). Originally a cattle market, it became known as a site for gladiatorial combats.

The women's goddess: A divinity associated with chastity and fertility. Her mysteries were closed to men, as was her real name, hence she was known simply as the Bona Dea (Good Goddess). The politician Publius Clodius Pulcher, brother of the Clodia who is thought by many to be Catullus' Lesbia, notoriously gatecrashed the Bona Dea rites, disguised as a woman, in 62 BC. He was discovered and eventually brought to trial, but was acquitted, reportedly as a result of bribery of the jurors.

Propped up the globe: Hercules once temporarily took the sky (or in some versions the earth) on his mighty shoulders from the giant Atlas (see note to III.22).

Alcides: Son (or rather grandson) of Alcaeus, father of Amphitryon, husband of Hercules' mother Alcmena – except that Hercules was sired by Jupiter (see note to II.22), an incident that gave rise to Juno's hatred of Hercules, mentioned in this poem. There may also be an echo of the Greek word *'alke'* (strength). The earlier reference to Hercules' 'less than god-like words' alludes to his half-divine, half-mortal status.

Stygian gloom: Another of Hercules' labours was to capture the underworld hound Cerberus. He also killed the Nemean lion, whose mane (mentioned a few lines further on) he then wore round his neck. Hercules refers to the fact that the labour to acquire the apples of the Hesperides took him to North Africa.

Lydia: On Hercules' temporary enslavement to the Lydian queen Omphale, see note to III.11. His talk of cross-dressing, along with a similar remark by Vertumnus in IV.2, have provided rich pickings for gender studies in Propertius' work. Hercules sometimes appeared as a figure of fun in ancient literature, including Aristophanes' *Frogs* (405 BC).

Tiresias: He accidentally saw Minerva bathing and was blinded as a consequence, but was consoled with the gift of prophecy. In mythology, after Perseus killed the Gorgon Medusa, he gave her head to Minerva to put on her shield.

Cures: See note to IV.4.

Sancus: A Roman god associated with trust, honesty and oaths, who had a temple on the Quirinal Hill. The first-century-BC Greek historian Dionysius of Halicarnassus says his worship was imported to Rome in early times by the Sabines. Several ancient authors identify him with Hercules. There are doubts over the text here, however, and some scholars believe the penultimate couplet is spurious.

IV.10

The subject is the temple of Jupiter Feretrius, supposedly founded by Romulus and situated on the Capitoline Hill, where it was rebuilt by Augustus. Here were stored the prestigious *'spolia opima'* (literally 'rich spoils') – arms and other trappings that a victorious Roman commander stripped from the body of an opposing leader whom he had killed in single combat. Propertius details the three occasions, beginning with Romulus, when this was recognised as having occurred. Some ten years before his poem was written, the proconsul Marcus Licinius Crassus personally killed a Carpathian ruler in battle, but was denied the *spolia opima* on the grounds that his command derived from Octavian. The incident shows Octavian's sensitivity to kudos going to anyone but himself. Propertius offers his own etymology of the name Feretrian at the end of the poem, but its true significance is not known.

Acron: The king of the now disappeared Sabine city of Caenina led a reprisal attack on Rome following the Rape of the Sabine Women (see note to II.6).

Cossus: Aulus Cornelius Cossus, consul in 428 BC, killed Lars Tolumnius, king of the Etruscan city of Veii, about ten miles northwest of Rome, of which it was an early rival. Tolumnius had initiated a war against Rome that ended with Veii's destruction.

Nomentum ... Cora: Sabine towns. The 'three acres' was the amount of land given to each Roman settler following the capture of Cora.

Claudius: Marcus Claudius Marcellus, an ancestor of the man whose death is lamented in III.18. In 222 BC he defeated a Gallic force at Casteggio (ancient Clastidium) near the modern Italian town of Voghera (what is now northern Italy was regarded in ancient times as part of Gaul). Virdomarus, the Gallic leader that Claudius slew, is identified as such by his 'Belgian' shield, his torque (a neck ornament) and his trousers – a garment whose wear, as Roberto Gazich notes in his Italian translation of Propertius, was 'unknown to the Romans'. On **Brennus**, see note to III.13.

IV.11

Paullus: The speaker from beyond the grave is Cornelia, a historical character who was daughter of an otherwise unknown Cornelius Scipio and of the much better known Scribonia – later married for a time to Augustus (making Cornelia the emperor's step-daughter). Cornelia married Paullus Aemilius Lepidus, a senior Roman politician. A mention that she died in the year of her brother's consulship (16 BC) would give us an approximate date for the poem, indeed for the publication of Book Four, but some scholars have questioned whether the couplet in question is authentic. The poem is a kind of expanded tomb inscription, addressing Cornelia's widower and children, but is also a rhetorical self-defence before the judges of the underworld to ensure her an honoured place in the next life.

The boatman: Charon. See note to III.18.

Aeacus: In Greek mythology, Aeacus and his half-brothers Minos and Rhadamanthus were judges in the underworld, determining the treatment accorded to dead souls. The Furies, who pursue the guilty, are also portrayed as present, but elements of the scene reflect Roman legal proceedings.

Sisyphus ...: See note to II.17. **Ixion** was tormented on a wheel. On **Tantalus** and **Danaus**, see note to II.1, and on **Cerberus**, note to III.5.

Spanish bronze: Rightly or wrongly, Propertius descends Cornelia from both the men known as Scipio Africanus, who won major victories against the Carthaginians (see also note to III.11). The younger Scipio also destroyed the city of Numantia in the Tarragona area of Spain – at one point considered a threat as great as Carthage – in 133 BC.

The king of Macedon: Propertius also descends Cornelia (wrongly, say scholars) from Aemilius Paullus, who in 168 BC defeated Perseus (not to be confused with the mythological figure of the same name) to end the kingdom of Macedon in northern Greece, whose most famous monarch was Alexander the Great. Perseus claimed descent from the Homeric hero Achilles. I have paraphrased an almost certainly corrupt manuscript text.

Claudia: A statue of the goddess Cybele was transported from Asia to Rome in 204 BC, but the ship ran aground in the Tiber. Claudia managed to free it, an action seen as proving her chastity, which had been called into question. Similarly, Aemilia was a Vestal Virgin, on whose watch the sacred fire in Vesta's temple appeared to go out, laying her open to punishment. While praying to Vesta, she placed part of her dress on the altar, which caused the fire to flare up again, vindicating her.

Garments of a fruitful spouse: Women who had three children were entitled to wear special clothing.

Afterword

When today's readers think about the great Latin love poets, they probably think of Catullus, whose intense chronicle of a failed affair has struck a chord in modern times; or Ovid and his hilarious manual on seduction techniques; or even Horace, with his wry reflections on life from his country retreat. One writer they may not think of is Propertius, who was part of the same poetic wave in the first century BC and whose best work competes with anything produced by the others, but who has been treated less kindly by posterity. This book seeks to go some way to correcting that bias and to make a case that Propertius has something to say to us.

What little we know of the life of Sextus Propertius is based mainly on deductions from things he himself says in his poems. He was born in Umbria, central Italy, probably in or near Assisi, whose most famous son he was until eclipsed by St Francis more than a thousand years later. Roman inscriptions kept in the town museum make clear the Propertius family was prominent in the area. In the nineteenth century, a Roman dwelling was excavated under the church of Santa Maria Maggiore in Assisi and was dubbed the 'House of Propertius', although there is no proof that it belonged to the poet's family. The main evidence is a Latin graffito, which – thanks to the precise Roman system of dating – we know was scrawled on a wall there on 24 February, AD 367, and which says: 'I have kissed the house of the Muse'. Researchers have taken this as a reference to Propertius and have speculated that the house was a kind of tourist attraction four centuries after his lifetime. A rival claim from the nearby town of Spello to be the poet's birthplace is now largely discounted.

From a reference he makes to the time when he assumed adult male clothing, something Roman boys did in their mid-teens, the date of Propertius' birth is usually put in the 50s BC, which was approximately when Catullus died. In 41 BC, the region plunged into violence when forces loyal to Octavian, later to become the Emperor Augustus, laid siege to the city of Perugia, not far from Assisi, to put down a rebellion. The revolt related in part to confiscations of land to provide farms for veterans who had fought on the winning side in the civil wars that had long convulsed the Roman world. Poem 1.22 tells us that Propertius lost a relative in the fighting, while Poem iv.1 says his family had some of its estates appropriated, reducing its wealth. The poet's father died around this time. His mother sent him to study law in Rome, a normal first step in a political career for well-born men. But Propertius had no taste for politics, and dedicated himself to poetry.

His first book of verse has long been dated to around 29 BC, although Peter Heslin, who has written the introduction to this book, has argued in a separate article that it was probably published somewhat earlier, before the watershed Battle of Actium (31 BC). Propertius' second volume (which some experts think in its present form is a conflation of two books) seems to have come out in the mid-20s, his third by about 22 and his fourth and final book in 16 or 15 BC. His poetry was clearly highly popular and soon brought him into the circle of the famous literary patron Maecenas, a close aide of Augustus, and certainly also to the attention of the emperor himself. The date of Propertius' death is unclear. Some assume it must have come soon after 15 BC, but I am not the only reader to see clear signs in the poet's fourth book that he had written himself into a dead end. The American author John Williams, in his epistolary novel *Augustus*, imagines Propertius in about 10 BC as having given up poetry and retired to his native Umbria. In any case, by AD 1 or 2, Ovid is referring to him in the past tense with the implication that he is dead.

The decades immediately preceding and following the transformation of the Roman Republic into an Empire were marked by an extraordinary upsurge of poetic talent – the four writers I have mentioned, plus Vergil, Tibullus and others whose work has survived only in fragments or not at all. There is a striking similarity with another historical turning point nearly two millennia later – the Russian Revolution of 1917: think of Blok, Yesenin, Mayakovsky, Tsvetayeva, Mandelshtam, Akhmatova and Pasternak. And, as with that period, those engaged in the apparently harmless pursuit of personal poetry soon found themselves at odds with a regime demanding public art that would promote its political agenda.

The Republic, governed for centuries by a Senate and two annually elected consuls, staggered through decades of civil conflict between rival warlords until it finally collapsed. On 2 September, 31 BC, at the naval Battle of Actium off the west coast of Greece, Octavian routed the fleets of Mark Antony and his Egyptian ally and lover Cleopatra. The way was clear for the victor to establish a new political order.

The date also marks a clear fault-line in literature. The Republic may not have been a democracy as we now understand the term but Catullus, its principal love poet whose work has survived, was able to write passionate lyrics to the well-known wife (if it was she) of a prominent politician as well as rude epigrams lampooning Julius Caesar. Those were not options for his successors, as the price of peace in Italy turned out to be the loss of many civil liberties that had existed before. Augustus progressively introduced totalitarian rule and policies that included the 'family values' programme that has been dear to dictators of various epochs.

Reading through Propertius' work leaves little doubt that he (among others) was on the sharp end of these policies. He wanted to write love poems; the regime wanted him to write panegyrics on Augustus, or at least something dealing with Roman history and its triumphal progress towards the Empire.

Propertius' initial reaction was to resort to a traditional *recusatio*, a disingenuous protestation that he was not up to grand themes. In this he cited the precedent of Greek poets he admired such as Callimachus, the leading light in the Alexandria-based Hellenistic school of the third century BC. But by the time we come to his fourth book, he had been forced to compromise: he would go half-way to meeting official demands for poems in praise of Roman history by writing 'aetiological' verse (from Greek '*aition*', a cause) on the origins of religious practices or buildings of his day. There is a notable parallel with Horace, whose fourth book of *Odes* appeared only a couple of years later, suggesting official pressure was building at that time. Both men give signs of trying to resist becoming poets-laureate. But Horace looks more willing to 'render unto Caesar', and a number of his later poems can only be seen as straight adulation of Augustus and his military conquests on the far-flung borders of Roman-controlled territory.

Today's reader may ask what Propertius' real attitude was. I concur with Professor Heslin, that he was far from being the committed imperialist some scholars have portrayed, although neither was he an open political dissident. His compliments to the emperor are often back-handed and even in Poem IV.6, which describes Actium, he distances himself so far from the action that it is hard to imagine the imperial court would have been satisfied with it. My impression is that his resistance was primarily literary: he felt that anything he wrote along the lines the regime was demanding would prove to be what Catullus had memorably described as '*cacata carta*' – 'shit-covered paper'.

Political changes also affected those poems (the bulk of the hundred or so he published) that on the face of it have nothing to do with public life and concern a relationship with a woman he calls Cynthia. Few readers have been able to avoid wondering who (or what) Cynthia was.

Again, it helps to look first at Catullus and his poems about 'Lesbia', the name he gave his beloved in homage to the seventh-century-BC Greek poet Sappho of Lesbos. His audience would have known that in reality (as most – though not all – modern classicists have accepted) she was Clodia, the wife, and later the widow, of the politician Metellus Celer, and a figure who crops up elsewhere in Roman literature. More than twenty centuries later, the love story recounted by Catullus still makes perfect sense: from initial infatuation through doubt to despair and anger.

By contrast, the Cynthia story makes far less sense. The only piece of information we have about her comes from the second-century-AD writer Apuleius, author of the fantasy novel *The Golden Ass*, who says in another work that she was really called Hostia – a name suggesting she came from a prominent Roman family. (The name Cynthia is linked to an epithet of Apollo, the patron god of poetry.) This has been increasingly disputed by scholars. While a few think she may have been an upper-class wife, most believe she is meant to appear as a '*meretrix*', usually translated as 'courtesan'. In today's terms, she comes across much of the time as a sort of self-employed escort.

Furthermore, it has proved impossible to construct a coherent chronology of an 'affair' between her and the poet. The details Propertius supplies of, for example, how long they have been together, are contradictory. While literary historians and translators once took his declared passion for her at face value, the prevailing view in the academic world nowadays is that she is a composite figure of his imagination; in short, that she did not exist. Some see her in 'metapoetic' terms, as a symbol of the sort of poetry Propertius wanted to write. What seems clear to me is that Propertius was more or less compelled to present her in this way in the new world in which Augustus was promoting marriage, child-bearing and chastity (of women, at least) among well-born Romans. For a poet, it was now safer that a beloved should be of dubious social status and uncertain identity, somewhere in the no-man's-land between literary tradition and real life.

There are signs, especially in the earlier poems, that Propertius was groping for a new context in which to place love poetry. Possibly he was influenced by Lucretius' scientific epic *De rerum natura* (*On the Nature of the Universe*), which promoted the view of the Greek philosopher Epicurus that love, beyond the straight satisfaction of the sexual urge, was a kind of transient and sordid madness. In any case, when we read that Cynthia has gone to the country, or that the poet has been shipwrecked on a desert island while trying to get away from her, there is no expectation that we should take these as historical events. They are dramatic scenarios. But what many of these poems are really about is insecurity, jealousy, or obsession in relationships – and these are very real emotions. Elsewhere Propertius explores, sometimes in whimsical fashion, such issues as whether love can survive the absence or death of the beloved, the relationship of anger and violence to love, and even whether one should take all one's clothes off to make love. It is his psychological acuity that seems to me his true contribution to the genre.

Attempts to identify Cynthia would not matter greatly were it not that, of all the women who appear in the pages of the Roman love poets, she is, in my view, much the most fully and subtly drawn. By the end of the poems, we feel we know her, real or otherwise. And if we wonder why the narrator should be so concerned about the fidelity of a woman who may have been simply an up-market prostitute (or she about his), we should perhaps look at the heroines of nineteenth-century operas like Giacomo Puccini's Manon Lescaut or Giuseppe Verdi's Violetta in *La Traviata*. I will leave the last word on Cynthia's reality to Austin Warren, co-author with René Wellek of the influential *Theory of Literature*. Warren wrote in an essay on Robert Herrick: 'Does any artist, whether novelist or poet, either draw literally the people he has known or not draw upon observation?'

A few years after Propertius' death, Ovid was permanently exiled by Augustus to the Black Sea coast of what is now Romania for reasons almost certainly connected in part with his spoof didactic poem *The Art of Love*, seen by the emperor as seriously off-message. The lesson cannot have been lost on other poets. Ovid's own death effectively marked the end of the short personal poem, barring an attempt by Martial to resurrect it in the second century AD in the form of epigrams. Between the first verses of Catullus and the last of Ovid, barely seventy-five years had passed in the many-century history of Latin literature.

One of the main obstacles that has come between Propertius and a modern appreciation of his poetry is his constant citing of Greek myths that were familiar to his contemporaries but are mostly not so today. Professor Heslin discusses this point in his introduction, and at much greater length in his recent book *Propertius, Greek Myth, and Virgil*. To help readers, I have written notes on the poems that provide background on mythology, Roman history and other matters not obvious to a twenty-first-century public. These appear in a separate section following the poems, where they may be consulted or not.

It is not my wish to burden the reader with another disquisition on the theory of verse translation, but, given Propertius' remoteness in time, it may be useful to say something of my own approach, in order to address issues raised with me by friends and acquaintances who have seen early drafts of these poems.

All of Propertius' extant poetry was written in the metre known as the elegiac couplet (described in the introduction). Like all classical Latin verse, it was unrhymed. Samuel Taylor Coleridge's version of a couplet by the German poet Friedrich Schiller gives an idea:

In the hexameter rises the fountain's silvery column;
In the pentameter aye falling in melody back.

But Latin metres were based on syllable length, an effect
which cannot be reproduced in English, and not on stress, as
is the case in modern verse (including the lines just quoted).
For this reason, and because the stress-based elegiac couplet
has proved monotonous in English when used for page after
page, I am not aware of any full version of Propertius that has
attempted it. I have not either.

Instead, the traditional measure for translating Propertius
into English was long the heroic couplet (iambic pentameters
rhyming AABBCC, etc.) Like the elegiac couplet, it tends to
make the unit of sense two lines, but I can see little other
similarity. For one thing, as Schiller indicated, the hexameter
is stronger than the pentameter in elegiacs, whereas in the
heroic couplet the second line is stronger as we build up to
the expected rhyme. Furthermore, in English literature the
heroic couplet is the metre *par excellence* of such poets as
Alexander Pope and John Dryden, and suits the kind of poetry
they wrote. But Propertius is a very different poet, writing a
very different kind of verse. The heroic couplet does not, in
my view, have the flexibility the elegiac couplet had in classi-
cal Latin. I have used it in just one poem, the last, to symbol-
ise its apparent surrender to the Augustan ideology of wifely
virtue, consigning to history almost everything Propertius
had written about Cynthia and his relationship with her.

A minor earthquake struck the Propertian world in 1919,
when Ezra Pound began to publish his *Homage to Sextus
Propertius*, written two years earlier. Pound had originally told
friends it was intended to plug the gap created by the lack of
a good translation. Written in twelve sections, it varies be-
tween a translation and a loose adaptation of parts of some
twenty of Propertius' poems. It was immediately derided by
classical scholars on the grounds of mistakes they said Pound

had made. For instance, '*canes*', meaning 'you will sing', is rendered by Pound as 'dogs' (which the Latin word can also mean). Classicists accustomed to correcting ignorant schoolboy 'howlers' could not imagine that Pound's mistranslations were anything else. The idea that he might have done them on purpose for his own effects did not occur to them. Wilfred Rowland Childe, a minor Georgian poet, sneered that the work was 'so full of egregious blunders that a fourth-form boy would be whipped for the least of them'. Readers of avant-garde English poetry, on the other hand, reacted cautiously. Most of them were unfamiliar with Propertius and could not quite see what Pound was up to. But the work has steadily gained supporters, some of whom consider it one of his best.

Pound replaced rhyme and metre with his own brand of muscular free verse, not unlike that used in his main original work, *The Cantos*. Here are a few lines (based on Poem III.1):

Annalists will continue to record Roman reputations,
Celebrities from the Trans-Caucasus will belaud Roman celebrities
And expound the distentions of Empire,
But for something to read in normal circumstances?
For a few pages brought down from the forked hill unsullied?
I ask a wreath which will not crush my head.
And there is no hurry about it;
I shall have, doubtless, a boom after my funeral,
Seeing that long standing increases all things
regardless of quality.

Pound's metrics reinforced his reading of Propertius as an ironist rather than the Catullus-style romantic poet of passion he had long been seen as – a view I share.

I have started from the belief that, despite the efforts of Pound and a number of subsequent translators, Propertius undeservedly remains a relative unknown among poetry readers today. In recent decades, he has attracted the attention of adherents of the theories of the twentieth-century French psychiatrist and philosopher Jacques Lacan and of feminist scholars interested in the gender implications of his work. But these studies have largely bypassed the broader public.

For all my admiration for the *Homage*, it would be folly for me to cast myself as another Pound, or to try to 'complete' his work, and I have attempted neither. Every translator needs to find his or her own voice. I should stress that this is not a literal version designed to help those with a little Latin to work through the original. Several excellent prose translations exist that serve such a purpose, the most easily accessible probably being the Loeb edition of George Goold (1990), which has a facing Latin text. Instead, I have essayed a verse translation based on the impossible (and yet somehow only possible) premise that Propertius were, as has been said, 'alive and writing in English today'. In other words, I have – at risk of serious *hubris* – tried to produce poems that can, despite the gulf of time separating us from Augustan Rome, work for the modern reader. Above all, I have sought to bring out the personality – ironic and at times subtly humorous – that I find in the original.

Sometimes I have hewed fairly closely to the Latin, at other times I have felt the need to be more adventurous while still seeing my work as translation, not adaptation or imitation. I have further imagined that, even though Propertius used a single metre, were he writing today he would employ a variety of forms, as suggested by the subject matter and tenor of each poem. Thus, the reader will find here free verse, but also some use of rhyme, half-rhyme and various types of metre or rhythm.

A word on place names. Like most translators, I have used English forms where these exist – Rome and Athens, for example. Slightly more controversially, where there is no separate English spelling, I have used the modern forms current in the countries concerned (mainly Italy), rather than the ancient versions. I have considered that Perugia is more likely to be known to readers than Perusia, and Modena than Mutina. Most controversially of all, I have occasionally used the names of countries that did not exist in the same form in classical times, such as Turkey, Albania and Afghanistan. I have employed ancient names only in cases where either there is no human habitation now where towns or cities once stood, or where the historical name is the one that is generally understood. It would be perverse to speak not of Troy but of Hisarlik, the Turkish village that now stands on the site.

The numbering of the poems (if they originally had any titles, these have not survived) follows the order in medieval manuscripts, our earliest source. Cases where the manuscripts give as one poem what are now thought by scholars to be two account for numbers like 11.26a and 11.26b. The opposite situation accounts for such numbers as 111.24–25.

This book could not have come about without Michael Schmidt, Director of Carcanet Press and General Editor of *PN Review*, which first published some of these poems. He was willing to gamble on someone whose only previous contribution to world literature had been wire-service news stories with a maximum life expectancy of twenty-four hours. As I made the transition from news agency journalist to verse translator, he also gave me the benefit of his tradecraft acquired over more than forty years as a practising poet, critic and editor, suggesting improvements and turns of phrase.

I need to acknowledge those who taught me Latin and ancient Greek, in particular the late Robert Levens of Merton College, Oxford – himself no mean translator of some of Catullus' more outrageous epigrams.

In my teens, two books fired my interest in Latin poetry. One was *Poets in a Landscape* (1957) by the great classicist Gilbert Highet. Some of his literary judgments now look dated, but his enthusiasm for his subject (including the links between the poetry and the land of Italy) continues to shine through. The other was *Latin Explorations* (1963) by Kenneth Quinn, especially the chapter on what he terms the crisis in Roman personal poetry. Again, I don't agree with all his conclusions – I think he underrates Propertius, for example – but his determination to treat poetry as poetry, not anything else, is something I find lacking in many of the innumerable books and articles that have been written on the subject more recently.

As I worked on these translations, I was fortunate to receive assistance from some of the foremost Propertius scholars in the UK. Not having spent my life as a professional Latinist, I thought it advisable to follow a single edition. I have essentially been guided by the 2007 Oxford Classical Text edited by Stephen Heyworth, Bowra Fellow in Classics at Wadham College, Oxford. I believe mine is the first full English verse translation to take advantage of his edition, as well as his monumental commentary, *Cynthia*. Professor Heyworth has also discussed with me some points of detail on the text. He and Tristan Franklinos, Fellow of Trinity College, Oxford, also took time out from busy schedules to check through and correct my notes. For whatever faults remain in them, I am solely responsible. Peter Heslin, Professor of Classics at Durham University, kindly wrote the introduction to this volume and has also, in correspondence, illuminated a number of aspects of the poet's work.

My friend the Carcanet poet Jeffrey Wainwright, like me a part-time resident in Propertius' home region of Umbria (where many of these translations were done), has provided valuable help and advice over a period of years.

A special place goes to Ezra Pound's daughter, Mary de Rachewiltz, who entertained me to tea at her castle in the South Tyrol and enlightened me on her father's approach to translation. Her Italian version of a selection of Pound's work, done in consultation with him, includes one of the *Homage* poems.

Others who gave me comment and encouragement after reading some of the poems include: Cathie Alexander, Susan Armstrong, Ian Cathrow, Alison Finch, Pamela Gagliani, Ann Jefferson, Marcia McKean, Frances Reader, Bill Ross, Rona Skene, Janice Viarnaud, Ouida Weaver, Susan Weil and the late Mike Bygrave.

My greatest debt is to my wife, Tricia, to whom this book is dedicated, and our son Alex, who both urged me from the outset to pursue what must have seemed at first like an improbable enterprise.

Viepri, Italy, 2006 — Cambridge, England, 2018